Don't Come Crying Home

A Boy's Life in Dr Barnardo's Homes

WILLIAM FELL-HOLDEN

Matador
9 Priory Business Park
Kibworth Beauchamp
Leicestershire LE8 0RX, UK
Tel: (+44) 116 279 2299
Fax: (+44) 116 279 2277
Email: books@troubador.co.uk
Web: www.troubador.co.uk/matador

ISBN 978 1784621 407

British Library Cataloguing in Publication Data.
A catalogue record for this book is available from the British Library.

Printed and bound by CPI Group (UK) Ltd, Croydon, CR0 4YY
Typeset in Book Antiqua by Troubador Publishing Ltd

This work is dedicated to Ollie and Toby,
and to the memory of Robert "Bob" Peach

CONTENTS

CONTENTS

PROLOGUE

'I can't believe it's 'im – the great man hiss-self!'

'It is. I wouldn't 'ave missed this, not for all . . .'

'Mile End I've come from. 'Ere, want a samwitch?'

'No, thank you.'

''Ere, you getting posh for the occasion then?'

They both laughed, pushing together with the crowd, as they all stared up the empty road.

'Fancy a man like that, from the classes, doing all that work.'

'Tell me, ducks, he picked them up from the gutter.'

'And the gables, they say.'

The crowd grew hushed, in the distance a black block moved slowly; coming into view, it could be seen by the present onlookers that the funeral procession was accompanied by various officials and loyal, tidily-dressed boys and girls from the care of the deceased man's Homes: Dr Barnardo.

''Ere, just thinking: Dr Barnardo hiss-self is lying there; 'un what a mis'rable day ter bury 'im.'

'Yer right there Alice, we can't stand in this rain all day. 'Ere, I wonder if he's got 'is top hat on?'

They both giggled.

'No, 'is was a religion yer could understand. Gawd bless 'im, 'elping all those homeless little 'uns.'

'Yer right there, Alice. It's a sad day for all those orfuns. What will they do now?'

'Don't know about them, Maud. I got ter get ter see to me little nippers, they need their mother. My old man says, "Don't be late now".'

'Come on Alice, let's get away a'fore the crowds catch us.'

It is Wednesday the 27th September 1905, the date of the funeral, and since the 17th September, the day that Dr Barnardo died of a heart attack, in his sixtieth year, the great man has been lying in state at The Edinburgh Castle, the gin palace he changed into an Evangelical Centre, in the district of Limehouse, London; there his body rested, for the mourning of the nation.

This day, "The Ever Welcome Door" had a shadow cast over it: the Founder had departed; may he rest in peace.

It was a month later, in that same year, up in the North of England, many miles from the start of Dr Barnardo's Homes in the East End of London, that Gladys was born. She may well have been a candidate for Dr Barnardo's but for the concern of the putative father's family; not, I may add, for Gladys, nor indeed, for her mother, Ann Elizabeth. The concern was not even for the reputation of the father – he was unknown, but was rumoured to be the son of a major mill owner from Lancashire; there is no one now to tell, yet one could continue to conjecture…

'Now, Ralph,' (it could well be imagined) spoke the wealthy mill owner to his son, while the latter meekly sat on a comfortable heirloom chair, upholstered in the very cotton created by his weaver women, and the former stood, legs akimbo, in all his social status, before the large open-hearth fire, 'you can thank your lucky stars that that young lass works for the business. It's all seen to – she'll be set up in one of the cottages (and it will be a mile or two out from here). Of course, when she's able she must work at something or other in the nearest mill, to pay her rent. There's nothing free in this world – you'll find that out soon enough.'

'Father…'

'You can't see her again – nor the little brat.'

'It's a girl.'

'Ay, that's as may be. You must not get attached. You've sown your oats – now you settle down, and do your future farming with better stock. You follow my meaning, son?'

'Yes, father.'

That was the generation that bore a daughter to Gran (who, latterly, was a domestic servant in the mill owner's service). Gladys was born on the 13th October in the year of 1905. She was to be my mother, in the springtime of 1941, having borne my brother, eighteen months previously, both by the same married man, a respectable person of the community, and both out of wedlock.

Such are the ways of men, be they king or porter.

PREPARATORY

'Get away with you, you can't be going to the mill with that belly on you – over eight months, and no one sees you've a bun in the oven? Daft I call it!'

'Yes, well if the old fella just came that time and collected the rent!'

'Collect the rent? I'll give him "rent collector"; more like he left a deposit – you'd better get some rent from him!'

Leave Mum alone, Gran – it weren't her fault! If only I was born then, even before my brother and I could think to speak up.

'Ay, there's the mill hooter – make up your mind; Muriel next door can go and tell the foreman: you needn't go.'

And she didn't.

The doctor came and delivered of Gladys my brother, Edward, remarking: 'You have done well on your first baby!'

And another summer came – and nearly went: unfortunately for Gladys the rent man came too, out of his usual routine, and went a-walk with mother and child (that was the gossip in the village). Soon enough, 'true to form', as the neighbours repeated to each other, 'Gladys is up the spout again! You can guess who by – and she's not married to him!'

Draw 'round in dust the broken wing.

Djuna Barnes
(Miranda) *The Antiphon*

1

BORN

The weaver's cottage had a busy time that afternoon. The blossoming apple tree boughs, the birds singing in the small garden, the sun full-shining on the hollyhocks, the bees filling the spring air with buzz, and inside the Doctor remarking: 'Ay, you have turned out a fine one. Or should I say number two!'

So I was born, and not aware of my eighteen-month brother; indeed, not aware of much; not the one visit by my father, or later the daily absence of my mother out at the cotton mill early each morning, with only Gran to care for us, and she almost blind; and unaware of the struggle she and Mum had to make ends meet. My mother had asked the local chapel to help in the care and upkeep of her children. The chapel's minister had referred her request to the local representative of Dr Barnardo's Homes. From there the ball of events started to roll; this led to my eventual departure to the guardianship responsibility of the Christian-imbued Homes. My awareness came with the shock appearance of the outside world, two summers and more months later: the morning I was taken away – from my gran and my mother, and my bigger brother, and the village cottages that huddled around my home.

*

Early September 1943 Correspondence
(Dr Barnardo files)

Letter is from the Barnardo Manager(s) to Rev. Cornthwaite of the Evangelical Protestant Church, Ribchester, Lancashire.

> With reference to your letter of the 28th ult., as the child in whom you are interested is of illegitimate birth, and only help from the Auxiliary Boarding-out Fund is contemplated, it is not necessary for such detailed information to be supplied as in the case where admission is to be considered. At the same time, we like to have as many particulars as possible concerning the mother and the putative father and of the mother's record, but answers to many of the questions concerning the child may be omitted. It is hardly necessary to give details as to uncles and aunts. As indicated, we like to know the mother's story, and the circumstances leading up to the child's birth.
>
> Yours very truly, (unsigned) Secretary to the Managers (Dr. Barnardo's).

*

6ᵗʰ September 1943 Correspondence

Letter to Rev. Cornthwaite from Barnardo's ('the Managers'?)

Dear Mr (Rev) Cornthwaite,

With reference to your letter of the 4ᵗʰ instant, I am sorry there should have been any misunderstanding about this case.

As a matter of fact we are not generally prepared to take the younger of two illegitimate children, although, until further information is available, I do not want entirely to shut out the possibility of our doing so. In this instance, I am afraid when I wrote to you on the Int.[1] instant I did not realise that there were two children. Even so, as I have indicated, it would not be customary for us to admit the younger one, but our help would more likely be by way of the admission of the elder child, assuming he or she is still dependent upon the mother.

However, I did not wish to put you to any trouble in the matter, and I think it would be a good plan if I were to ask the Birkdale representative of the Homes, the Rev. J. R. Brightman, to take the matter up with a view to collecting such additional particulars as would be required where a decision could be arrived at.

Yours truly, (unsigned).

*

(Dr Barnardo files re Applicant)

Name & Address of applicant: Pastor T. Cornthwaite, Elmfield, Ribchester Road, Clayton-le-Dale, Blackburn.
NI No. of candidate: INBA/314/- *APPLICATION FORM.*

Holden, Eric 3.4.1941 Ribchester. *Not legitimate. Not baptized.*
Mother and child at 28 Blackburn Road, Ribchester, Preston, Lancashire.

Child did not attend Sunday school. Did not attend day school. Not attended school for mental or defective children.

General health: *Good.*
Had or subject to fits? *No.*
Had measles? *No.*
Scarlet Fever? *No.*
Whooping cough? *Yes.*
Diphtheria? *No (immunised).*
Smallpox? *No.*

No other malady or physical defect. Mental capacity: *Average.*

Mother's details: Holden, Gladys. British. Age 35 years. 28 Blackburn Road, Ribchester, Lancs.
Occupation: *Weaver. At W. Smith, Longridge, Preston. Member of Weavers Union.*

General health: *Good.*
Religious denomination: *C of E.*
Weekly rent paid: *13/- (13 shillings) including rates. Mother willing to contribute to best of her ability.*

Brothers: **Holden, Edward. Age 4 years. c/o 28 Blackburn Road, Ribchester, Lancs.**
Sisters: *None.*
Grandparents: (Maternal) **Simpson, Elizabeth Ann. Age 67 years. 28 Blackburn Road, Ribchester, Lancs.**
Uncles and Aunts: *No natural/material[1] relatives.*

Has candidate ever been convicted? *No.*
Has candidate ever been in the workhouse?[2] *No.*
Information as respect to the candidate's character, habits and disposition, and whether the candidate's habits are clean:
Normally behaved, generally obedient; occasionally W.B. (wets bed).[3]
Will full Agreement be signed by parent? *Yes. By mother.*

Background Information of Applicant.

Family History of Candidate.

The applicant in this case, Pastor T. Cornthwaite, has been the minister of the Evangelical Protestant Church, Ribchester, near Preston, for nearly thirty years. The members of this small but progressive church have been good supporters of Barnardo work for very many years and they would, I am sure, be encouraged if the candidate, born at Ribchester two and a half years ago, were in due course admitted to the Homes. Mr Cornthwaite explained that the mother has lived in the village for the past four years and has now two illegitimate children (by the same father). She does not attend the church, but many of the church people have taken a practical interest in her case. Despite her lapse, she is felt to be worthy of what help the Managers may feel able to offer.

In the course of her narrative, the mother stated that she was born in Preston and lived there until removing to Ribchester in 1939. The maternal grandfather died when the mother was about six years old; later the grandmother re-married, but the stepfather died when the mother was fourteen. Upon leaving school at the age of fourteen, the mother worked as a weaver for ten years at one place of employment; then for the next six to seven years she worked, also as a weaver, at another place. The putative father, who was living apart from his wife, used to call for the rent of the house in which the mother lived and, becoming friendly with the mother, he made overtures to her which she unwisely accepted. Concerned lest news of his behaviour might leak out and prejudice his position as a police officer, he made arrangements for the mother and grandmother to move to Ribchester a few weeks before the child Edward was born. He gave the mother financial help, urging her not to take proceedings against him.

When Edward was six months old, the mother obtained work in a Ribchester weaving shed, the grandmother meanwhile having the care of this child. Unhappily the putative father visited the home from time to time and thus it came about that for a second time the mother became pregnant. This second child (the candidate) was born at Ribchester, 3/4/1941, the putative father paying all the expenses of the confinement. He has not called to see the mother since October 1941 but he sends occasional payments for the maintenance of the children.

Sometimes he may send £3 or £4 – then after a period of two or three months he sends further assistance. Thus it may be that on the average the mother receives 5/- (five shillings) a week from the putative father. Should the candidate be admitted to the Homes, the mother states that the putative father should be willing to give a written promise to pay some agreed sum for the maintenance of the child.

For the past two years, the mother has worked at Longridge, near Preston, her wages being on the average £3 per week. She leaves home for work at 6.50 a.m. and returns at 5.40 p.m. The children are left in the care of the grandmother, but although she is willing to do her best, she is almost blind and cannot, therefore, give the children the care that they need. This fact is a constant source of worry to the mother, who seems to be most devoted to both her children.

The grandmother's income is small: 10/- per week Old Age Pension and 7/6 per week Blind Person's Pension. It follows, then, that the general expenses of the home (food and rent, etc.) are paid by the mother from her earnings.

It must be noted that the candidate is the younger of two illegitimate children: both in the applicant and to the mother the general rule in cases like this was carefully explained, as set out in the letter sent to the applicant on September 8th (reference C/WSW/ 266454). The mother said that if the Managers offered to admit Edward, she would feel compelled to decline, on the grounds that this boy is of a nervous and highly strung temperament and would probably fret dreadfully if he went away from home. My observation of this little fellow led me to agree with the mother's view, for Edward seems to be exceptionally shy and frightened; the candidate, on the other hand, appears to be much more normal in behaviour.

Is it possible, therefore, to consider the younger of two children as the candidate in circumstances such as these? For the sake of all concerned I amend this case to the Managers for their sympathetic attention.

(Signed) John R. Brightman.

*

5th October 1943 Correspondence

Dear Rev. Brightman,

Re Eric Holden

This case has now had our careful consideration. We feel, however, that the mother should take proceedings against the putative father, or arrange for him to enter into an agreement to contribute a regular sum per week for the children's maintenance. In view of the eldest child's temperament, we are willing to stretch a point, and offer to receive the youngest child, Eric, on condition that the putative father's payments are transferred to us, and also on condition that the mother herself contributes towards the child's maintenance at the rate of 5s. per week.

*

Dear Mr Lucette,

Re Eric Holden

In answer to your letter of the 8th inst. reference C/DW/ELH/266454, I write to explain that I wrote to the mother on October 11th telling her of the conditions in which you are prepared to receive this boy. So far I have heard nothing from her, but the delay may be due in part to the fact that she is getting into touch with the putative father and arranging with him to make a payment regularly toward the support of both children.

As soon as possible I will communicate with you again on this subject.

Yours sincerely, (Signed) John R. Brightman.

*

Letter to Dr Barnardo's Homes: Head Office. November 1943.

I have enclosed a list of Eric's relatives: his grandparents, uncles and aunts.

From: Rev. Brightman.

Letter to Rev. Brightman. November 1943.

We do not need such details of the boy's relatives +, only his mother and (putative) father is sufficient.

+ *(NB.* Therefore none recorded in files)
From: Admissions, Head Office, Dr Barnardo's Homes.

*

*(Form signing of **Agreement** to the passing over of the child from the parent(s) to the Guardianship/Care responsibility of the Dr Barnardo's Homes).*

DR. BARNARDO'S HOMES: NATIONAL INCORPORATED ASSOCIATION
STEPNEY, LONDON, ENGLAND,
and having Branches in

Bedford, Bedfordshire; Bristol, Gloucestershire; Belfast, Ireland; Liverpool and Birkdale, Lancashire; Birmingham, Warwickshire; Bromborough, Cheshire; Harrogate and Hull, Leeds, Middlesbrough, Ripon and Sheffield, Yorkshire; Crowborough, Hove and St. Leonards, Sussex; Cardiff, Glamorganshire; Kingston, Surrey; Exeter and Plymouth, Devonshire; Felixstowe, Suffolk; Folkstone, Hawkhurst and Southborough, Kent; Barkingside, Waltham Abbey and Woodford Bridge, Essex; Hertford, Hertfordshire; Llandudno, Carnarvonshire; Newcastle, Northumberland; Northampton, Northamptonshire; Washington, Durham; North Elmham, Norfolk; Portsmouth, Shirley and Southampton, Hampshire; Parkstone, Dorsetshire; Much Wenlock, Shropshire; Toronto, Ontario, Canada; Sydney, New South Wales, Australia; Pinjurra, Western Australia, together with

BOARDING-OUT CENTRES *in rural homes throughout* ENGLAND, *in* ONTARIO, CANADA, *and* NEW SOUTH WALES, AUSTRALIA *and* WESTERN AUSTRALIA.

An Agreement made this eighth day of November one thousand nine hundred and forty-three between Dr Barnardo's Homes, National Incorporated Association, 18 to 26 Stepney Causeway, E.1 in the County of London, of the one part and (Miss) Gladys Holden of 28 Blackburn Road, Ribchester, Near Preston the mother of Eric Holden hereinafter called the NEXT FRIEND of the other part.

Whereby it is agreed as follows: (1-7 Clauses)

1. The NEXT FRIEND hereby hands over the said child to the charge of the MANAGERS of the said PROSTESTANT HOMES to be taken care of maintained and educated in any of the Branches named at the head of this Agreement or to be BOARDED-OUT by the aforesaid MANAGERS in the United Kingdom or Canada or Australia as the MANAGERS shall decide.

2. The NEXT FRIEND agrees that the said child shall be under the Guardianship of the MANAGERS until the said child shall attain the age of twenty-one years or for a shorter period if the MANAGERS think so and that during the whole

term of the said child's residence in the said Homes or Branches the said child shall be brought up in the PROTESTANT FAITH.

3. The NEXT FRIEND hereby gives consent to the said child being transferred to Canada or Australia if the MANAGERS think it desirable.

4. The MANAGERS on their part undertake properly to maintain, educate and train the said child in one of their Branches or boarded-out in the United Kingdom or Canada or Australia so long as the said child shall remain in their custody.

5. The NEXT FRIEND shall receive back the said child into her care in case the MANAGERS of the said Homes for the time being shall for any good cause require the said child to be removed from the said Homes.

6. The NEXT FRIEND shall not before the expiration of the period mentioned in the second clause of this Agreement remove the said child from the care of the MANAGERS without having first obtained the consent of the MANAGERS for the time being and in case the NEXT FRIEND shall before the expiration of the said term remove the said child with the consent of the MANAGERS the NEXT FRIEND shall previously to such removal repay to the MANAGERS as and for the expense

of the maintenance and education of the said child the sum of six shillings per every week during which the said child has resided in any of the said Homes or Branches or been boarded-out as aforesaid together with the cost incurred (if any) for the travelling expenses of the said child to and from the aforesaid Homes or Branches or Boarding-Out Centres.

7.   The NEXT FRIEND also gives willing consent to the said MANAGERS to send the said child at any time they may think proper to any person's care or home or situation or place of employment which may be provided for the said child other than at the above-named BRANCHES whether at home or abroad, whether in the UNITED KINGDOM, or in ANY of HIS MAJESTY'S COLONIES, DEPENDENCIES, or DOMINIONS OVERSEAS.

(Mother duly signed the Agreement Form and thereby signed away her responsibility for me, to that of the Guardianship and care of Dr Barnardo's Homes.)

*

10 November 1943 Correspondence

Dr Barnardo's Homes: National Incorporated Association
18 to 26 Stepney Causeway, London, E1

The Superintendent,
Ever Open Door,
16 Trafalgar Road,
Birkdale,
Lancs.
Dear Mr Lucette,

Re Eric Holden

In answer to your letter of the 8th ult. reference C/DW/ELH/266454, I enclose herewith the completed Agreement form with the putative father whereby the latter will pay 5/- per week for each child; the 5/- paid for the candidate will be transferred to us by the mother as you propose. Further, the mother will herself pay 5/- per week for the maintenance of the candidate.

Yours sincerely,
(Signed) John R. Brightman.

*

17 November 1943 Correspondence
C/DW/ELH/266454

Dear Mr Brightman,

Re Eric Holden

Thank you for your letter of the 10th instant enclosing our completed Agreement in respect of the above-mentioned boy. We note that arrangements have now been made for the putative father to contribute 5s. per week towards Eric's maintenance and that this amount will be transferred to these Homes, also that the mother herself proposes to contribute 5s. per week for the boy's maintenance. I am pleased to be able to tell you that we have a vacancy for Eric at our Branch at Aqualate Hall, Nr. Newport, Salop – Superintendent Mrs Heard and I should be grateful if you could make the necessary arrangements for his transfer to that Branch, and communicate with Mrs Heard fixing a mutually convenient date for his reception.

It is essential that Eric takes with him his Identity Card, Respirator* and Ration Book, including Clothing Book and any available Coupons. He should also be accompanied by the enclosed Freedom from Infection certificate duly completed by a Doctor.

Yours sincerely,
(Unsigned)

*Wartime gas mask supplied to civilians.

*

4th December 1943 Correspondence

BIRKDALE Early Open Door Home

Dear Mr Lucette,

Re Eric Holden

In answer to your letter of the 17th ult. reference C/DW/ELH/266454, I write to report that this transfer has not been overlooked, but so far I have not found it possible to arrange for the boy to be escorted to Aqualate Hall.

Probably within the next fortnight the transfer can be made, but the matter is made more difficult owing to the fact that from the 4th. to the 18th. inst. I am away on leave and, moreover, a new Matron is just about to take over her duties at this Early Open Door Home. I will do my best to make the necessary plans as soon as possible.

Yours sincerely,
        (Signed) John R. Brightman

*

17 November 1943 Correspondence
C/DW/ELH/266454

Dear Mrs Heard,

Re Eric Holden – born 3.4.41

I should be glad if you will arrange to receive the above-mentioned child when you hear from our representative at Birkdale – the Reverend J. R. Brightman, 16 Trafalgar Road, Birkdale. I have asked Mr Brightman if he will kindly communicate with you, fixing a mutually convenient date for the child's transfer.

Eric is described as a normally behaved child and generally obedient; he suffers occasionally from enuresis.

The next of kin is the mother, Miss Gladys Holden of 28 Blackburn Road, Ribchester, Nr. Preston.

I enclose the usual Dossier Card, also slip regarding Ration Book etc. for completion and return after Eric has been received by you.

Yours sincerely,

(Unsigned) Mr Lucette, Head Office.

Mrs Heard, Aqualate Hall.

*

2

BARNARDO YEARS: AQUALATE HALL

At first he would not take interest in nurses being in the room with him.

'Here's the child, Rev. Brightman; he'll settle down.'

I was bawling away – who wouldn't at two years of age? This was my second passing over to a stranger – and I had never before been outside the place that was my home.

'I am sure he will,' the Reverend replied to the departing health worker.

So, I was transferred from one stranger to another. I sat, I cried, I nestled into the coat of my temporary guardian: smokiness and stale tobacco was my last memory of that new journey. It was wartime, December 1943.

'The small child slept all the way. He's had a long trip, all across Shropshire. I will leave the child's documents.'

'Well, thank you, Rev. Brightman. He is a sickly-looking thing.' Mrs Heard took me in her arms and stood me down beside her.

The door shut on Rev. Brightman and the outside world. It was the beginning of my incarceration: from now on, for the next nineteen years, I was a Dr. Barnardo's Boy – a "Barnardo Boy".

'You can stop your snivelling for a start – follow me.'

I toddled beside her, dazed and numb. She was a woman, a mother figure, yet I wasn't getting a feeling of comfort from her. Strange: the pattern for my future behaviour was here being laid on me; the web I was given the task to sort out later now began to weave.

Mrs Heard's legs were large. I couldn't see further than her swirl of skirt. She moved as a mighty tank. She smelt as the kitchen we entered, musty, dank and dark. Her voice was as uninviting as the cold, beige tiles of the walls.

'Get your bottom down there.' She pointed to a child-size, three-legged stool. My heart was hardening. I had to protect the precious inside of me – to keep safe the small sunshine of my lost paradise.

'You don't say much, do you? I hear you were a noisy little brat on the train. Well, we don't tolerate that sort of stuff here.' She slapped my face. I couldn't cry. Well, my first response was to holler. I held back. This was a war I was forced to enter. I learned here my first conscious lesson of survival: how to repress my feelings.

'You needn't look so shocked. You'll be getting plenty of them while you're here.'

She rustled through my documents: 'Eric Holden – huh, that's what we'll stick to here: no lovey-dovey "Eric". You're a bastard – no fancy words from me. That's what you are; and a second one too, I see! Your mother a whore; it certainly looks like it.' She slapped my face a second time. 'I'm Matron here,' she told me.

My eyes watered. I didn't understand her words, what she was reading out. I knew only her care for me was unkind; her voice hard. I desperately wanted to cry: my sharpening instinct guided me not to do so. I tightened my lips.

'Plucky little bastard, aren't you? Better give you some supper.' Mrs Heard opened cupboards high above my stool seat level. 'A bit of bread and jam do you no harm.'

Hearing familiar food words, my body sagged in weakness. I hadn't eaten for several hours; sleep had passed my time. My body let out its hunger: 'Yes', my first word on coming inside the Home. It was small, barely audible in the vast empty kitchen.

'You can speak can you? Bastard boy…'

'That the new arrival, Matron? Oh! Isn't he puny? His bed is ready. Shall I toilet him?'

This voice belonged to a young person. She had on a white apron. She looked like a friendly helper. She was not as big as Mrs Heard.

'Give him his bread!' Matron instructed, and left the kitchen; she glanced at me, a distasteful expression on her face: 'He'll be a little devil I'll have you know, Jane – a little devil.'

'What's the red marks on your face?' The helper bent down and put her plump face near mine. Her fruity-smelling breath heaved out. 'Have you been a naughty little boy, Eric Holden? That won't do. Matron doesn't like naughty boys.'

I began to understand that "naughty" and "bastard" had a linked meaning. I was taking in the education of my new being. My mind had started to know, so early in my life, that I was a thing, a separate human being: that I was "different" – and less than other human beings.

'Here, little Eric Holden – "little Eric", that'll be my pet name for you.' She smiled. I was happy at such a sight from another woman here. She was friendlier than the Matron. 'Take your supper.'

I ate the jam sandwich on my stool – and another. I drank the cold milk. This liquid was difficult to swallow. I discovered I didn't like milk. I would develop the ability to take many other things I didn't like, to give the appearance of acceptance, while inside, my body repressed and bricked up the small voice of choice.

Mrs Heard noted in one of her Home reports:

At first he would not take interest in nurses being in the room with him.

He would take no interest in me or the nurses but still clings to my hand if there is a stranger in the room.

3

ILLNESS AND THE MENTAL QUESTION

Tall and thin for age; healthy physically. Gait bad.
Very nervous. Mentally very backward.

Night was as strange as the day to me at Aqualate Hall; the empty echo of the vast dormitory, with cots and beds jutting out from the walls. Other babies and toddlers were snivelling or sobbing, with shadow figures rustling between the inmates of this peculiar cold sleeping place.

I dreamed of the sumptuous-looking apples of my lost home; the hanging glow of the fruit. I dreamed of my granny and her warm smell, wrappings and wrappings of her blouses and clothes to snuggle up to; of the soft comfort of my Mother – and somewhere in the shadows, the shifting form of my lost brother. I awoke in the early morning, crying.

A strange tall lady appeared before me. She adjusted her small white cap: 'What's the matter?' I pointed to my tummy. 'Stomach ache? We'll get you on the toilet, sit up.' She went and got me something to drink – a teaspoon of a liquid, new to my senses. It smelt peculiar but oddly appealing.

I automatically opened my mouth. The teaspoon clattered on my small teeth. I swallowed. I choked. I coughed.

'Do you good. Swallow now.'

The sticky stuff hung in my mouth till breakfast time.

The babies in their high chairs – with flannel bibs, toddlers, such as me, in low down seats (I could barely reach my porridge bowl) and Jane moving about the edges of the table, helping here and there. The wood-panelled dining room was quiet – no child said a word; there was only an occasional burble from a baby. The distant clatter of the kitchen and the autopilot expression of Jane, and her voice, repeating every now and then: 'there, there' – usually accompanied by the intrusion of her chubby fingers into the small eating world of a child struggling with his spoon in his dish.

I did not remember much else about this Home, Aqualate Hall. That is, after the first shock of entry and of coming up against the powerful Mrs Heard – and my struggle, always, at resisting her attempts to punish and control me.

My records revealed that I had just missed, by the skin of my teeth, some kind of mental institution. Mrs Heard had written to the Home's Medical Officer:

> This child refuses to eat; is dirty and a bad influence on the other children. He is backward and mentally deficient. He needs to be in a Special Home.

Letters went back and forth, to Head Office, to Enquiry Officer and from Mrs Heard:

Mrs Heard (Aqualate Hall) informed us of difficulties with this boy whom she thinks is definitely mentally deficient.

Dr Smith saw him on Saturday and will see him again on Wednesday.

Nothing to be gained at present on technical grounds in expediting action if child were mentally deficient… on psychological grounds we must not disturb a child until after a really lengthy period of observation.

Likely cause of child's present erratic behaviour is distress at new environment to which we hope he will eventually become accustomed.

Letter to Mrs Heard, from Head Office, informing her (from our Enquiry Officer) that:

Eric was born in small village and from what mother said had seen very few people in his short life and had not travelled until day he was taken to Stafford. Boy was, not unnaturally, most distressed when mother left him at Preston Station, but calmed down and was soon fast asleep on Rev. Brightman's knee. Eric apparently screamed on changing hands again at Stafford.

It is Rev. Brightman's view that boy will settle down
in time and be happy member of Barnardo family.

Luckily, for my age, the Chief Medical Officer was
aware of the effects of emotional separation of very
young children, from their mothers, into an
environment that was alien and uncomforting:

He will settle down in time. I suggest his behaviour
is from the strangeness of his new surroundings.

That was his reply. And that was that, but Mrs
Heard's reports still complained of me: "Very spiteful
with other children". Even so, her other observations
noted that I had:

Bad attacks of vomiting. He is seen by Dr Smith
each week… Eric is a delicate little boy.

Detailing my appearance, I was a:

Tall but very thin, frail little boy; very highly
strung, backward and uncontrollable; bad gait; a
very neurotic subject.

And further observations:

Fond of toys and odd things such as handbags etc.
But will not join in with games; a bad companion
for normal children who copy all his funny ways.

Months after entering Aqualate Hall I had to go into a local hospital, Tithe Barn, because of scarlet fever. I returned back to the Home after one month of hospital care. It was noted in reports that:

> Eric is back again at Aqualate Hall and quite happy. Health, however, not as good as we would desire. Has had to be kept in bed a great deal since his return from hospital for stomach trouble. Receiving special attention and we hope to build him up into a normally healthy child... he will have special medical supervision.

By my Home's records I see that soon after I was shifted to another Home, one for toddlers only; one where the Matron was more understanding of me – and where my world opened up a little with a ray of sunshine, through affection.

4

ASHLEY COOMBE

*Eric was very nervous when he first came to us but
now is more at home. Difficult at times but
very much improved.*

28.3.1946   Letter to mother, Miss Holden, 34
Water Street, Ribchester, Preston,
Lancashire, informing her Eric now at
Porlock.

I had just turned five. I was aware of the satisfaction
of order at the sight of the clock tower and the
dignified frontage of my new Home, Ashley
Coombe, in Somerset.

This Home was set in large woodland. It had a
long arched walkway like a brick viaduct. This
reached high up into the main building, from the
side. Tall dark woodland grew on the upward slope
behind this decorative walkway. The whole vision of
this place, towering above me yet comforting and
embracing, had a peace for me, even as the humans
about my life were distant: they lacked the emotional
attachment which this place gave me.

Wolves howled in the night (in reality, probably
the Home's dog). And the lawns stretched, neat and

emerald, across my vision. Here, left to myself, I became confirmed in my own reality that I was a separate being, isolated in a world which had no emotional comfort for me. Though my records did state – under the signature of a different Head of Home, Mrs Robinson – that:

> Eric was very nervous when he first came to us but now is more at home.
> Difficult at times but very much improved.
> Eric responds well to affection.

There at least appeared a glimmer of joy, for my emotional wellbeing, yet my bodily health required to be attended to and watched for "special treatment". It was a year on from my entry into Barnardo's that Mrs Robinson wrote:

> Eric has so much improved in behaviour, that he seems a different boy.
> Definitely needs guidance and encouragement.

A year again, further on, and Mrs Robinson's reports describe my state:

> Has improved both physically and very definitely mentally. Thin type of child.
> Enuresis still present at times, it has improved but marked again since starting outside (Infants) school. Greatly improved behaviour. Difficult with

> some of the staff who do not understand him. Has
> an attaché case which he loves playing with,
> wrapping up little parcels etc. and carrying them
> in this case.

> Eric is the type of boy who likes to wander off and
> play on his own. He is affectionate, and a little
> affection and encouragement helps him very
> much. A refined looking child. Likes to work with
> his hands.

I think, on reflection, I certainly was often left by
myself, for I visualised in those early Homes days
standing high up on the wide, long stairway, and
gazing down into the hall, contemplating the sight
of toddlers in simple buggies, and the bustle as staff
prepared to take the children for walks; it was all
happening apart from me; my Home-life role was
becoming that of "a loner".

'He's always in his thoughts, that one,' the
cleaning lady would chide to one of the carers that
dressed like nurses. 'He's got an old head on his
young shoulders, if you tell me,' she would continue
– then off she would go on her chores. And I, hearing
her words as more portent drops upon the wrapped-
up mystery of my being, stood, listened and observed.

So my days were spent seeing the empty
greyness of the backyard; the busy nurses; the flat
expanse of lawn; the walks about the grounds and
the vast emptiness of the moonlit night. I observed it

all but it did not belong to me. These scenes had not any emotional meaning for me. I was distant from the life blood of this home. Not that this life lasted for long; the next home would enliven me. It was the year 1947, and my mother requested a move for me – from the South of England to the North "to be nearer Eric, so I can visit him".

9.1.1947   Mother Miss Gladys Holden, 34 Water Street, Ribchester, Near Preston, Lancashire, asks if it would be possible for Eric to be transferred to home nearer her part of the country to enable her to visit him.

3.2.1947   Letter to mother (29.1.47) informing her we will bear her request in mind when a suitable vacancy arises but we are having considerable difficulty in finding places at the moment and it may be some time before we can move Eric.

3.3.1947   Placement decision: (Relatives want Eric nearer them. Mother lives near Preston. In 1946 it was stated in the Home report that boy was difficult at times; definitely needs affection, guidance and encouragement.) To Liverpool after Easter.

17.3.1947   Letter to mother (29.2.47) informing
              her of our hopes to transfer Eric to
              Branch (Home) at Liverpool (16
              Alexandra Drive) as soon as possible
              for her to visit him there but might be
              well to allow a few weeks to elapse
              after transfer to give him time to settle
              down. No doubt she will let us know
              in due course if she wishes to make
              application to see him.

The day came (yes, even a solitary child has attachments) when I was smartened up in shorts and shirt, neat in socks, sandals and combed hair, and ushered, whispered to, and friendly-pushed, into the dark fearful hole of a shiny black taxi-car. The day was sunny, my tears were falling, and the dark red roses glared on their bushes along the orange-brick wall. These were the last images of my second Home.

Soothed in the back seat, by the close comfort of another human being, a motherly woman, I travelled to… where?… Well?… where? I cannot remember, except the large lady in the back seat; she gave me warmth… and gentleness flowed in her smile.

They knew that my next Home would be a shift of many miles: from Somerset to Lancashire.

5

16 ALEXANDRA DRIVE, LIVERPOOL

Eric will be transferred… mother informed.

Liverpool: the broken down concrete wastes; the parachutes descending in slow motion; the one-penny glass of orange at the corner shop. The whole expanse of a new life opened up to my six-year-old brain. My eyes took it all in; my heart beat to a fresh and lively rhythm: this was life. Moments of running alongside the green-painted railings enclosing the playground and peering in at all the children shouting, laughing, crying and playing; of having a large coin held tightly in my hand and walking up the long cobbled street to the distant corner shop, and pushing through the faded brown doors and reaching up to the high counter and asking for, 'a penny orange, please.' And lifting down a full, cool glass of orange drink; of gulping it excitedly – giving the man back the glass, way above the wooden counter and running out of the shop, heart-bursting with happiness and freedom. I had moved to another place; to another Home. I had been "transferred," and my "mother informed." That year's Home Report duly stated:

5.5.1947	Mother granted permission to visit Eric at Liverpool on 31st May. (Mr Clarke, Superintendent, Liverpool, informed accordingly.)

Mr Clarke told me one day in springtime: 'Your mother will visit you today.'

A large lady in a dark coat met me as I was guided into the Home's hallway. 'Hello luv; how are you?'

'All right.' I hesitated, waiting, not knowing what I should be doing now.

'Say, "Thank you", Eric, and go out with your mother for the day.'

'Thank you.' I kept still. I ached with tension, anxious that I still didn't know what to do. Mr Clarke left the hall: just me and my mother standing opposite, looking at each other. She took me out – to Sefton Park; got me a sandwich later. We sat on a bench; I was uncomfortable in my clothes, my pullover made me sticky, and the day was very warm. My mother talked but I could not gather much from it. And the visit ended. I returned to my familiar place, in the Home, amongst the other boys. I knew my mother visiting was supposed to be important but she was a bit of a stranger, tagged onto me, and I was relieved when she left.

*

One day, a surprise visit of a creature to the classroom: 'Look, Lucy has brought a baby hedgehog to school.'

So it was 'Let's look!' and eagerly I saw a small black-eyed prickly thing, wrapped over with cloth, in Lucy's wicker handbasket. 'What ya gonna do with it?' I asked.

'Don't know. Show teacher.' And the small gathering of children made their way into morning school, and the teacher said to take care of it and return it to the park at lunchtime.

Playing with Barbara and Julia in the school yard – these two playmates I recall – was pleasurable. I was, for a short time, growing into security. I was forming friendships, emotional ties.

Christmas, and cone-shaped hand-size paper containers with sweets and one large orange given to us, were the memories of my Liverpool Infants School.

The Dr Barnardo's Home, near the big, sloping park, was home to me. My feelings were attached to the privacy of the black-painted iron fire escape at the back. There, by myself, I would play in the dust and enjoy the sunshine. Such privacy was another place of security – as was the high long wall which enclosed the large house and its tree-held gardens. Not far away to walk was Sefton Park, its open spaces, woods and lakes were fun for our little orphanage group. 'Look at that lady's hat!' I shouted, as it flew and rolled in the wind and skidded down the grass bank. That image of freedom was joyful for me, seeing, no doubt, the small tightness of emotional safety that locked my heart from feelings for other people. 'Let's run and catch it.' And I ran off down the slope, without the House Parent's assent, laughing and gurgling on the breeze.

Liverpool had its other attractions too: days on the bomb sites were intriguing times. Low concrete hut-size buildings – shelters I suppose, and broken lumps of white stone lying about them. We would scramble around and over them. Days too, when men jumped out of barrage balloons in the sky and slowly, timelessly, settled into the distant crowds of watching people, to disappear in the ruffle and whiteness of their parachute. Watching them I could not understand why they were doing it; though I knew it was some kind of "show".

Later, across the empty flat wastes of the fairground, after the fair and stalls had left, there a friend (no face, no name, a shadow of companionship) accompanied me. We, in great excitement, scavenged across the worn grass for cigarette packets and such debris rejected by adults.

'Here's one!' I would, excited, pick up a squashed red packet, with a black cat pictured on it, and hold with our other finds: a small coin, a badge. So off we'd go – free and wild – though how, at six years to seven years of age we got out of the house and achieved our freedom, I don't know.

At times we wandered to the dockyards, the

massive ship hulks towering above and in front of us. The giant rats (so they seemed to me) in cages; the complex, overpowering activity of the scene, all-consuming to my senses. This is the real beginning of life, my whole being told me; it was so till 1948 when the Home closed for us boys; we were all shifted – up and away.

> 22.4.1948   16 Alexandra Drive to be a Girls'
>   Home. Eric with the other boys will
>   be transferred to Home near Kendal.
>   Mother informed.

Farewell Barbara and Julia. Farewell sentiments of park and gardens. Farewell newfound security; and the high, high wall. I scraped my fingers and ran them along the stones of the huge wall that hid away the larger structure of St George's Hall and the statues in the centre of Liverpool; and visits to the docks: the ships, and cages, and things... all these slipped by. 'We are all moving to a house in the countryside. They are just fitting the wall lights,' I told other boys, my imagination filling in the image of a haunted mansion in a dark wood.

And Liverpool was gone. All that business of daily life and personal activity, and school friends, left behind. Comfort, like a shaken-out blanket, would be chucked to the elements, becoming meaningless dust on the wind of change.

We packed, we were off, albeit with some

excitement, out from Liverpool, to the solitude of a large and dark-centred house in Westmorland. Up till now, in my small life, I had attached myself to three different sets of people – and had each attachment wrenched away; I was learning that the only safety was in the certainty of my own being. I could trust only myself, and not reveal any feelings.

6

BARROWS GREEN: JOY AND CONFUSION

*Thin boy of rather pert and impish appearance,
not robust. Ephedrine for enuresis.*

Another Dr Barnardo's Home: it is summertime. I am in the countryside, under a large oak tree, in a wide and sloping field; the orphanage, Barrows Green, in Westmorland. Looking up I see a thin silken thread, taut and hanging down. At the end of it is a twirling, skinny caterpillar. I am transfixed by this new experience: a creature, moving as I would do at play, swinging down on a rope; and above is the thick-leafed oak tree – and the warmth of the sunny day surrounds me. Only this moment is my entire world.

There the new Home sat, on a rise of its own land; many-roofed, with a lawn at the back, running to a ha-ha, its lead-lined windows glinted in the sunshine. Along its holly-shadowed drive, its surround of dense woods, and its solitary position on the hill, the house presented itself as a haunted place.

Inside, the candle holders on the corridor walls had just been replaced by electricity bulbs. Or was this picturing to my child's mind just the appearance of things? Or the conjured-up imagery through the dim corridors; the accompanying echo of the grandfather clock chimes; or the beckoning silence of the huge stairway, its balustrade in dark wood?

All the children, like campers at a newly discovered site, scrabbled about, and we began to make our mark: this deserted territory was ours. We did settle for a while on the lawn at the field side of the house. There we gathered the daisies. 'Let's make a daisy chain?' a boy suggested. 'Yes! Yes!' our voices agreed. We concentrated on picking the daisies, pinching a small gap in the stalk and threading the next daisy stalk and flower through. So we continued till a necklace of white daisies with their yellow centre decorated each of our necks. We giggled and admired them, sitting still for a time; least, till our attention moved off to other things, like a butterfly, on which we would jump up: 'Catch it! Catch it! Bet you can't!' And we could not, as it bounced on the air and away.

The setting around the Home was of fields, dotted with grey hen sheds. I saw a horse pulling a plough over the land rise. There was a farm nearby, and a lot of emptiness all about. This place, Mr Clarke told us, was Westmorland.

Mr Clarke was to become my visiting devil, my presented horror. It was his mad-man wide grin which towered above me, and his dark eyes staring into mine; he was the Master of the Barrows Green

Home. His report notes on me stated that I was "a highly strung, nervous type of boy; thin of rather pert and impish appearance, not robust." Of my behaviour, he described me as being:

> Very irresponsible and mischievous, tends to be disobedient and destructive when opportunity occurs. No very outstanding improvement can be claimed as yet.

Later on, he described me as, "Utterly undependable and restless and highly strung". At school, I was "behind and not a trier"; I was "still on Ephedrine for enuresis". By 1949 I had "Generally improved... occasional enuresis".

'Come now, boys,' (this Home, like all the Dr Barnardo's Homes I occupied, had male-only children) Mr Clarke instructed and, as usual, approaching us menacingly, his brown rotten teeth in a grimace of some imagined pleasure, his thin moustache, two dark lines above his quivering lips, 'get your tea from Matron'. I did not like the grey spit often appearing at the corners of his mouth.

He would pass by us with a flap of his beige corduroy trousers and beige safari shirt, rubbing his hands together; his expressed pleasure, no doubt a plan being hatched, or re-lived, in his mind. His quick short-step walk then, thankfully, would take his hunched presence away from our fearing eyes, and into the dim distance that led to his office lair, far along at the end of the ground floor corridor.

One Saturday afternoon, I was told to hurry up the wide stone steps, leading from the house-side path to the back cellar entrance. I was slow and sulky at being shouted at, and so displayed my resistance to instruction.

'Change your face. Get up here quickly!' The Master faced down upon me.

I started up the bottom step. Next moment I was lying on the pathway; I had flown through the air – been thrown. I got up and silently began up the steps again. The Master turned away his angry face and walked off, not bothering with me. I did not feel hurt anywhere – I was thin and light, and anyway, only a child. I soon forgot about it.

Mr Clarke became the instigator of mental torture to me. I had caused some misdemeanour – I do not remember what. I was sent to him. I stood before him in the polished, main hall corridor – he had met me even before I had reached his sitting room door.

'Now what have you been doing? Something very naughty, I suppose.'

I stood there, expectant and in fear. 'Don't know,' I whispered.

He grinned, showing his brown gappy teeth. He smelt strongly of tobacco. His dark hair was slick and flattened back over his crown.

'You know' – he lifted his arms, and joined his hands, rubbing them together, his hair-covered fingers incessantly intertwining – 'you will be hung on a cross, if you don't behave yourself. Your arms will be cut off and your legs cut off.'

I stared, open-face, in shock at the image he was creating in my mind – I knew all about the Cross, Jesus, his suffering and the Crucifixion. The image of hanging there, fixed, began to haunt my brain.

'Your eyes will be blinded and your tongue cut off.' He leered at me. I felt trapped as his eyes travelled over my body; they felt to be touching me every place they covered. Froth stuff was appearing at the corners of his mouth. 'And we'll cut off that small willie there.' He sniggered. 'Yes.' He thought a moment, still staring at me. 'Get back to the playroom now.'

He walked off, briskly, in small steps, away into the dim of the corridor. I stood, stunned. He couldn't have punished me more – now and in the future. I wandered away, more distanced from people and the normality of social intercourse than ever before; my mind barely hung on to the taut guy ropes of my Christian teaching, for my inner world was desolate. And in bed that night, my imagination could find no escape from my fate. I could not even cry – the limits of my mental being were fixed; I slept then, my body stiff with anxiety, my mind pained in fear.

But the morning came and the day took my attention over, and the previous day's trauma sank into my being. The routine, and its security of expectedness, gave the rhythm of life at Barrows Green. My companionship was the birds and creatures of the woods, fields and grounds, including the lawns and orchard; the small chicken shed with its dry stifling smell inside, and its flapping group of squawking hens fluffing up fallen feathers into my face (for I squeezed my way in one day, out of curiosity) also took my attention.

And the flower beds and gardens: all an expanse of cared-for abundance; though this space was no real comfort for the exchange of society, with the hub and flow of the city I had lost. Even a village would have shown me the weave of daily life: of relationships, of family-meaning, birth, marriages, and family death. I sensed that there was something other, out there – a place, an area, than the place I was now living in. I did not feel that I belonged here. I entrenched myself as an observer of this domain – it did not belong to me.

My Homes report, written by Mr Clarke, stated:

There is appreciable all-round improvement in boy. His enuretic trouble is much diminished and his nervous reactions are much improved.

* * *

This was a time, in my seventh year, that I went home to my mother and granny for Christmas:

22.9.1948   Letter to Mr Lewis (House parent),
             asking him to call on mother and let
             us have report on home conditions, as
             she wishes to have boy home for
             Xmas.

22.11.1948   Letter to Mr Clarke, Barrows Green
             House, informing him we are looking
             in the matter of boy spending Xmas
             with mother.

22.11.1948   Report from Mr Lewis, Liverpool,
             mother lives with maternal
             grandmother and home contains four
             rooms, two bedrooms. Mother was
             decorating one bedroom for Eric, she
             has a single bed for him; she will
             sleep with grandmother.
             Grandmother is partially deaf and
             blind, but house was clean and tidy.
             Mother is employed as part-time
             weaver at local mill, wages £3 p.w.
             (To Mr Clarke, Barrows Green,
             informed him Xmas leave granted.)

Of this home stay I have little memory, but happy
ones. Of moving back and forward in Gran's black
shiny rocking chair; of fascination with the open fire
centred in the black cooking range, of the living
room; of the cosy warmth of the cottage – and the

large form of my mother, for Gran was little. And so quick, my stay was soon over. I left with odd feelings: sorrow at leaving, but happy picturing the Home's busy life; confused too, why I had to go back to the Barnardo Home, when my mother and Gran were here – and without me.

* * *

Older boys were also at Barrows Green; younger ones were the likes of me, at around seven years of age, going up to boys of sixteen or even seventeen. There was plenty of opportunity for peer group exploration – and abuse from older boys; the wide grounds, fields and woods, all offered privacy and protection from the eyes of authority.

Attention on me started before I can really remember: it was the next Home Superintendent, Mr Savidge, commenting that he found me in bed the day he arrived, put there in the mid-afternoon hours. It was reported to him that I was isolated upstairs: '"for being rude" – you had your pyjamas turned back to front.'

Thankfully, Mr Clarke was not long in authority at this Home, and had been replaced by Mr Savidge. I could not quite believe that I would not see Mr Clarke again – that the new Master would *always* be here, in his place. 'Is Mr Clarke *really* gone?' I asked Master one Sunday afternoon, when I saw him standing quietly looking out of the empty dining room windows.

'Don't look so troubled.' Master stared at me a moment. I waited before him, feeling small beneath his much taller height.

'I assure you Eric; Mr Clarke has left for good. I am in charge of the Home now.'

I beamed a smile at Master; *he* was in charge of the Home now – Mr Clarke had 'left for good'. I felt safer now. I ran down the corridor, happy – and there was the freedom of the Sunday afternoon walk to come.

* * *

My earliest memory of sexual attention was when being around a small fire the older boys had made in the middle woods in a clearing, with deep dark spaces behind our backs and surrounding us. A small gang of various ages gathered: 'Let's see it, Eric.' All eyes and leering faces turned to me. I shrank into my sitting position; I knew they wanted something of me – and their attention, for some odd reason (I barely sensed), was on my willie. I resisted, said nothing, and shifted uncomfortably. But I had to show them – and they gazed, till I pulled up my shorts, with a wary eye kept on my fireside companions.

Of course, I had my fancies – if a little boy can have such attraction for older boys. Even as I followed such boys around, I was becoming what I had been shaped to be from my first experience of sudden detachment: an outsider, a loner. I was comfortable and safe in my own company; as I have said, the woods and creatures were my true friends. 'This is Barrows Green. You will like it here.'

Sometimes the house staff were happy, and the Home's atmosphere lightened up, as if everyone was glad the children were about. Such times, it seemed, fitted in with a ditty that was in the air, about the Home:

> *If I knew you were comin' I'd have baked a cake*
> *baked a cake, baked a cake*
> *If I knew you were comin' I'd have baked a cake*
> *Howd-ya do? Howd-ya do? How'd-ya do?*

This buzzed round in my head at the time, and I liked it: it seemed to match the sunshine and the freedom of the trees I saw as I gazed from my small dormitory window, having wandered upstairs to get some self-presence and stillness, in my own company.

Mockingbird Hill was another song I liked; the light and happy female voice of Patti Page made me happy too:

> *Tra-la-la, tweedle dee dee it gives me a thrill*
> *To wake up in the morning to the mocking' bird's trill.*

Miss Naylor, one of the female house parents, noticed me; she gave me attention, and she behaved kindly. I had feelings of friendship toward her because of her quiet nature: not loud-talking or telling children off all the time.

As well as Miss Naylor, there was another houseparent I liked: a bigger female, very chubby and motherly. In spare minutes of the weekend I liked to sit on the bath edge and watch as Miss Talbot rinsed out the bed sheets. I was transfixed by the strength and size of her forearms as she rung the sheet into tight furls letting out the clear water into the bath. She would smile at me watching her. Her nature was soft and this was a puzzle to me: that she appeared big and strong yet was gentle and friendly. And I never heard her shout at us, but she could be serious in instructing us some times. She let me be myself, which I liked – not demanding anything, or any particular behaviour, from me. It was between these two female staff that I wanted to be near, for they had care for me.

It was here at Barrows Green that I became conscious that I "wet the bed". I did not like the whole procedure of the orange-coloured rubber underlay being changed, and my sheet taken for washing. I had done wrong, I thought, as there was such fuss being made of it. Wetting the bed did not seem a regular occurrence, but I did it intermittently. 'Eric not yet suitable for adoption' would be written in my records. I later wondered if my bed-wetting was the reason. It was too late for any adoption a couple of years down the line, as I was "settling in": it would "be disruptive for Eric, as he gets on very well with the other boys". So that was that for the last opportunity of a conventional family life.

7

PLANTS, NATURE AND HURT

March 1949. Height: 47 ins. Weight: 46 lbs.
Dark brown hair. Grey eyes. Wiry type.
Slight, tall child.

Here at Barrows Green, I was surprised at the powerful blowing wind and all the space of sky and fields, and woods; and I noticed the loneliness. No bustle of people, no streets of activity – just space and me; but the vegetation and insects and animals and birds took over for people. By myself, I wandered, looking always at the back of my activity, sensing for something: maybe my lost joy from the Liverpool Home. But in nature I began to be more conscious of my being, as a separate self, for I was the observer, more so now. I watched nature and I watched my companions, the staff and the comings and goings of the Home. The "otherness" society was out there, and I was me, my only true reality. My world was my feelings and thoughts, and these I mainly kept to myself, for they were mine and precious, for all else had been taken from me. I was clothed as a stranger, fed as a stranger, taught, admonished and given religious instruction as a stranger; for this world, this society, was really someone else's; my meaning was only me, and that meaning I had to protect and defend.

My Home report of the year routinely stated my physical statistics:

> March 1949. Height: 47 ins. Weight: 46 lbs. Dark brown hair. Grey eyes. Wiry type. Slight, tall child.

Our weekday routine was to get up at quarter to seven, wash, have breakfast: cereal in summer and porridge in winter, a light-cooked course, say of sausage and tinned tomatoes, and a drink of some sort, probably tea. Then clean our teeth and off to Crosscrake School, this being the local primary, a good mile's walk: down the lane into a valley and up the hill and down again, onto a level where the small stone-built schoolhouse stood. It was surrounded by a high, grey, dry-stone wall, dotted here and there with small wild plants. Around it were sloping fields where curlews nested in the long meadow grass where, one time, I was dive-bombed by one of these large curved-beak birds as I searched for its nest in the grass. Further on from the school were one or two hamlets and a small farm.

From Crosscrake, at a later age, we went to the town's baths and there learnt to swim. The teacher of our class asked: 'Who can do the breadth now?' I waited quietly in the water, getting a surprise as my name, as if from a distance, reached my hearing: 'Eric Holden can do it, sir!' I could swim that distance and so, under the eyes of the whole class in the pool behind me, I set out and self-consciously swam the breadth of the baths.

'Well done, Eric,' the teacher said. 'Now everyone else try.' And so the usual noise of splashing swimmers returned my world to normal, once more in the pandemonium of activity. I felt proud for that time; I was different and I received acclaim for it.

In the large sparse classrooms we were taught to read and do simple maths. We heard stories from the teacher, enraptured, and sometimes listened to things from the headmaster's radio. We drank our small bottle of milk at morning break-time. In winter they were warmed, lined around the railings which enclosed the narrow stove; the dark-grey stove that stood off from the wall in the headmaster's classroom. We had plants that grew from seeds in jam jars, and a small caged animal lived in the classroom too. We sat on strict behaviour in rows of desks and only had any kind of freedom at playtime, country square dance, and when we painted. In fact the paint days were fun for me, though I had difficulty in understanding the release from adult control, on being told to paint anything we imagined, of the island where the Bong tree grows, where the owl and the pussycat landed from their pea-green boat (as the tale went). Such mental freedom I found it hard to manage. I strained to push my mind to grasp that island, or rather, to find escape from myself, with adult permission, to create a world in whatever way we liked. But the facts of the physical world, just paint and paper, pulled my mind to the plain play materials; even so, bright yellow, red and emerald green splashed onto the trees and soil of the island, and soon filled up the white space of my painting sheet. The exercise was satisfying: I had discovered that there could be other moments and ways of freedom in my life. I could add colour to them, through my imagination.

There was a girl, very self-contained, from "outside" (we Home boys, Barnardo's Boys were different from the normal family children; it was like we were looked upon as prisoners let out, but under some sort of control, and not to be socialised with by the children from the local hamlets, and certainly not from the well-off girls, like the calm, poised girl from one of the farms). I saw her once, in her out-of-school time, when we were having one of our walks from the Home. She was high up on a grey horse. She looked so self-composed … I couldn't give words to the mixture of feelings she stirred in me: I wanted to be like her; wanted to be her, sitting on that high-up pale horse, appearing to have a surety about her, which I too wanted to possess. I knew that I ached to be with her, wanted her just to talk to me, touch me, but she was unattainable, I could only look on, or rather up, to her. We would gaze at each other but never speak. She may have been a little older than me, though we were both at primary school at this time, of about ten or eleven years in age. From her position to me, I knew from that time that I, in my personal value, was really different: worth less than others, who were not from the Homes.

Yet another girl that reached the core of my childhood existence – a woman really, healthy-looking in her cotton summer dress, her full bosom motherly – who I saw sometimes, from the hamlet of Crosscrake, and had moved to live by the sea. I overheard a Crosscrake family woman say, 'It's such a shame; just left a week ago to live in Blackpool, and was run down by a tram.'

'Yes,' another woman from the small gathering added, 'killed, and such a young woman.'

This information shocked me; I could not relate how Beatrice, so full of life, could not be alive – and the image of her living in my mind, but not now a breathing person, perplexed me. I could not believe, did not want to believe, this sudden change of reality.

Yet my life went on. My reports recorded by the new Superintendent, Mr Savidge, stated that I was: "In good health;" but that I still wet the bed: "Nocturnal enuresis". However, things *were* changing in me: my behaviour was: "Good;" I had "entered the Cubs;" and played: "General small boy's games". I was: "Always smiling; Eric is full of life and appears to be extremely happy."

I had seen a large pale blue hydrangea in a pot on the Saturday market in town: 'Can I buy it with my pocket money?' I asked Master.

'Do you want to spend all your money on that one plant?'

'Yes,' I firmly stated, for I was determined to get it; the sight of the bloom took my heart.

Back at the Home, Master told me to go to the outer terrace underneath his office. *Good,* I thought, *I am getting all my pocket money savings.*

And sure enough, the office window opened above me and out came Master's arm and dropped several sixpences into my cupped hands below. I grinned and looked up: 'Thank you.' He closed the window and I scarpered off. Moments later Master met me on coming into the playroom.

'Come with me and we will get your plant.'

With more unexpected pleasure I followed Master to the Home's Austin of England dark green van, and we travelled the couple of miles to town.

The same pot with the blue hydrangea was on show, and I proudly bought it.

I got it home, holding it with care: a green and blue plant in a green van – all the way back. Proudly I displayed it on the wall top of the open back porch. It would be safe there, though I did not give that a thought, knowing the plant was mine. A globe of butterfly petals opened up all around.

Just down the porch steps, at the base of the grey stone wall, tall asters grew, with their tightly furled knobs of flowers, ready to open, and nearby, the jewelled faces of sweet william, which gave me pleasure each time I went up to them and sniffed at their lovely scent.

My joy and interest in plants grew and I was given a small plot of land at the back of the raised front lawn, behind its evergreen hedge. There I placed, in the scraped soil, small brown bits of seeds; the packet pictured large orange carrots.

To my great surprise and happiness, after a few days fresh green feathery leaves appeared where I had put in the seeds. It was amazing, the hope of my imagination was fulfilled, and from that moment I wanted to be a gardener.

Certainly I was happy with nature; my activities here were in watching and tracking birds, to find their nests, like the mistle thrush that flew frequently to the rowan tree on the driveway. I reached up to the first fork on the short tree and I received a shock. The bird darted down to me and swooped close, over my head. I knew it did not want me to touch its nest, so I left it alone. One weekend in the summer I got an old oil drum and put some sugar in a small bowl to entice bees, as I wanted my own beehive. I saw a bumblebee around the drum, but due to the busy days of my play life I forgot the hive, and only discovered it again, with some dead bees near it, the following winter. A happy discovery was a rabbit's burrow hole on the driveway bank which sloped toward the kitchen garden hedge. I managed to put my arm all the way down the passage and just at the end I felt the soft fur of a nest – and gently fetched out a small cuddly young rabbit. I put it back soon to keep it safe. Of course, I also tried to catch birds, this by using an old metal sieve, propped up with a stick, and tied to the stick, a long piece of string. If I quickly pulled the stick away with a bird underneath, I would have caught it. But my scheme didn't work. I think I was too excited about the whole thing, also feeling unhappy, imagining a trapped panicky bird, to want to continue with this particular experiment. Exploring under an old rusty corrugated sheet in the wood I saw the world of the shrew. One of them stayed in its runway, and I caught it, but quickly dropped it, with a shake of my hand, the instant it nipped my finger with its sharp teeth. The shrew's high squeaks had led me to their covered nest. Now I carefully placed the corrugated sheet back over it and the little tunnel runways.

I used to wander too, and the fields were my escape – they were also the place where I would be abused. We kept rabbits as pets and fed them mainly on young dandelion leaves. These were foraged by us from the fields which spread for miles from the Home grounds: grass stretches that were un-peopled and without animals – or so it seemed each time we explored over them, or travelled beside them, down the country lanes.

'Come on, we'll get rabbit food; I'll take the sleigh.' Dave Smitt, a bigger and much older boy than me, instructed me to accompany him. I followed without a word – even though it was more the habit for boys of our own age to play or do things, like collecting dandelion leaves, together.

I vaguely sensed something was up, but could not focus on what was making me insecure. The size of him and the power of his personality did not prompt any questions from me – such as why do you really want me to go with you?

We travelled over the near field of Howard's farm – a dog barked from work sheds, though we saw no one about. Across at least two more fields we went, and with Dave Smitt pulling the sleigh, I was having difficulty keeping up with his long strides. I wished to loiter; I could hear the skylarks singing as they climbed higher into the blue sky; I was getting tired, I wanted to lie in the grass, to watch the white butterflies and hear, close to, the buzz of bees over the buttercups, over the pale blue meadow flowers. I looked at the yellow cowslips, their flowers dangling and moving in the warm breeze – in them I sought some anchorage of past pleasure.

'Keep up!' Dave Smitt demanded, and I quickened my walk. We approached the viaduct which carried trains across the Westmorland valleys and on to some northern part, unknown to me. We entered the small tunnel underneath: 'Pull your shorts down. Lie there.'

I did as instructed; and for a moment enjoyed the cool air around my bared belly, even though the ground was stony and pressed into my back.

Dave Smitt got down, his long legs each side,

straddling me. He knelt, pulling my body along, closer to him; his size leant over, suffocating the space between us. He pushed up my shirt further. The tunnel breeze flowed cool on my legs, and cooler still as the rest of my body became naked, by Dave Smitt's hand, completed by tugging off my shoes and socks. I shivered. An instant picture of my full nakedness came and went, in and out of my whirling imagination. His big boy's body blocked out the light; it weighted a great pressure on me. It all happened fast; overwhelming moments passed, without time, yet time drew slowly over my senses. My only awareness, a hard pressure poking, and poking, into my belly; and it hurt. After this pain, my mind filled with blackness; it centred in that dark emptiness; it had no thought or image; no line, or spark of light. Into my nose came a strong porridge smell. After that I forgot everything: the weight, the darkness, and the smell. I came round feeling light and free: he had gotten off my body; I saw his legs standing by me.

'Get up.'

My senses quickly came together on hearing his full voice; I got up. It was difficult to hold my balance. I was weakened. I was confused; power, like an electric shock, had entered my being and I could not figure out what had happened.

Dazed, I wobbled on my legs to a standstill, my shorts around my ankles and my shirt open and bedraggled. At some stage, he must have tried to put back on my clothes. I stood, at a loss, not knowing my presence. I shivered. My tummy was wet.

'Pick up your shorts then.'

I followed his instructions, my movements slow and uncertain. I tucked in my loose shirt and struggled to put on my socks and shoes. I was dressed enough to be warmed. At my eye height, I saw him buckle his snake-head belt. He leaned down and collected the rope of the sledge with its small pile of dandelion leaves. He looked down into my face. I gawped at his large, open eyes, caught by their power. 'Follow me, and don't come crying home; we just picked leaves for the rabbits, ok?'

'Yes.' My voice sounded weak. Confused still, I could not reply otherwise. He stared at me.

I won't cry. I won't cry. I pictured the Home, and the other boys, free and happy, in the playroom.

We left the shade of the railway arch and entered the bright sunlight. Over the field I stumbled. The ground, like my mind, slanted this way and that, its previous balance gone; it kept in its own confusion; a bolt of something had shot through me, and something of it remained, locked inside of me.

On our way back, we collected more dandelion leaves. 'Just break off the fresh ones,' he kept on saying, and telling me: 'Just the small ones.' My mind righted itself to take in the sunshine as we walked, slower than the hurried way we came, over the fields. I could breathe again, but somewhere inside of me my heart had been pressed to a smaller place.

Over the field near to Howard's farm, their dogs barked. I pictured last summer's visit there, when the son called me into the yard: 'Watch the haymaking.' I did, standing by the huge stone barn. I envied their son – same age as me, yet was allowed to drive their small tractor on the farm. But the sunny haymaking day ended for me after seeing one of their collie working dogs get trapped against the barn upright by a wheel of the machine. It yelped in pain; only moments ago it was frisking around us. I walked away, feeling the peace of the scene had altered, and that I should not now be there. But I was happy that day: with the hay stalks and dust flying through the air; the heat of the afternoon; and all hands alive with farm life activity.

Soon all the day's images slipped from my mind in the ache of my legs. It was a long and tiring walk returning to Barrows Green that afternoon; at times I rubbed the itching where the belly wet was drying. Master stood at the open kitchen window on our entering the bike yard, beneath him: 'You're late back. Is the boy all right?' He looked at me. I stared back, silent.

'Yes, he's just a bit tired walking.'

'Let him go to rest in the playroom.'

Master met me in the back corridor, by the kitchen door. 'Are you well?' he asked me.

'I feel a bit not well.' I hesitated to say more; for I could not explain anyway.

'Come with me.'

He took me with him, holding my hand, up the main stairway. This was unusual: these stairs, in their wide polished wood steps and bannisters were for Master and Matron; we boys used the back stairs, opposite the kitchen.

'You rest in bed. Get into your pyjamas and I will get you a warm drink.' He left me at the dormitory entrance. I changed into my night clothes. This seemed to take a while. I moved in a sluggish dream, half-conscious of what I was doing – partly thinking of the bed and the drink to come.

Master came in; I had almost fallen asleep. 'Here, drink this; then go to sleep.'

'Thank you.' I took the warm beaker. Inside was tea. It smelt warm. I sipped its sweet and milky comfort. I put the beaker onto the side locker, lay back, and the day left me as I slipped into sleep.

I awoke in the darkness. All the beds were full of boys. It was night. I had slept till now and wanted the toilet. I got out of bed and by the dimness of the corridor night-light I made my way to the bathroom toilet. Master was there. I didn't look up at him but went to the toilet as he was doing too. He had on his long pyjamas; his willie was at my eye level, it stuck out, long, over the basin; I weed beneath him. Neither of us said a word. I finished and returned to my bed, glad that Master had been there with me.

Back into the routine of the Home I soon forgot the happening of a week ago; too much was going on in my daily life, and being so young. That day soon became a compressed memory, and a layer of deep significance for my mind – and my nurtured sexuality. Later it would build up to a sense of guilt and a need to control the demon inside of me. My primary school report at about this time stated that I had become "mopey".

This trip with Dave Smitt did have its repercussions in the Home: between the older boys I must have become known as being sexually available, for I was approached by others of that group from time to time.

In particular I was accosted by Peter – a dark-haired handsome sixteen year old, whom I did admire for his looks and friendly way.

We met in the narrow passage that curved its way from the washrooms to a side door – all at the work-a-day back area of the house. The bare rough concrete walls kept the passageway cool and funnelled any sound of approaching feet from the main house door quickly along to where we stood.

Peter pulled down his trousers; his private parts were suddenly shot into my vision – for I was at eyesight height from them. I saw his large dick – it had no specific conscious meaning for me.

'You've got a lot of hair,' I exclaimed, as at the back of my mind I wondered why he stood there, smiling, not saying anything. I didn't know what I was supposed to do – for it seemed he was waiting for something.

Footsteps sounded in the farther corridor joining the house: 'Quick, go away,' Peter said. And he left, in the direction of the house. I darted into the nearby communal toilet room. I stood there in the silence; all footsteps had gone. I peed into the long metal trough, finished, and moved over to gaze out of the open window, looking down into the sloping area of the drive and across it, to the kitchen garden woods. It was safer, I understood, to wait a while before going back into the main house.

Staring at the trees, the thick camouflage of bushes and leaves, I was comforted; they were the cushion of my bewildering world – a world of an order not emotionally connected to me, a world of things and behaviour that ran a different course to my feelings, to my sentiment of what had value. I was conscious of my body – my whole person, a skinny child, in baggy shorts and shirt, becoming cold and uncared for in the shadows of the concrete toilet block, the steel urinal and four sit-down bowls my only company.

In the outer corridor, from the toilets, I met Smitt; seeing him shocked me to a standstill. He stopped, stared at me. I stared, transfixed at his legs. I desired to clasp them – something there, at the top, held my feelings. My breath caught in my chest and it came heavy from me. He smiled but I did not like how he looked at me. 'You had something with Peter then?'

I did not know what he meant. I reacted with a

yelp-sounding, 'No!' understanding there was something in his suggestion which I had to reject.

'Want to come with me again?'

My mind blanked. His big body was towering over me the moment I came to my senses. I looked up to his face. I knew that my eyes pleaded with him; the moisture there told me. He smiled again: 'All right, not now.' He turned away, going further down the corridor. My throat and tongue stuck as I tried to swallow. I shivered from the corridor air. Relieved that he was gone, I went up the stone steps, pushed the door open and escaped into the main house. Its dim passageway was my safety. The image of Smitt hung in my mind. It drew me to him, like I belonged to him. Yet I feared him also.

I was a stranger here, in this Home as in the previous ones – it was a world without human warmth for me. I looked on, nothing and no one touched my heart. Even occasional visits by my mother did not connect me to any social reality of a conventional kind. She, after all, was now a distant figure of less importance. She herself did not show me any physical affection; that was her life, how she was. My granny of course didn't come to visit: she was getting old and was poor in vision; I had pushed her affection deep inside of me, where what little of personal value I had was hidden, squashed to a silent corner, protected from further oppression and abuse.

8

BETRAYAL

Eric approximates a normal boy of his age but highly strung. Not suitable for boarding out.

Betrayal was the early course of my life: from adults, from other boys. Religion even, and its moral base, wasn't a safety net for my falling world. I had to begin to form my own view of what existence – my particular existence – meant.

Albert, another attractive boy, now well into his seventeenth year, was a beacon of moral uprightness. He spouted religious guidance to us younger occupants of the Home. He was about to join, or doing some type of training, for the police, or ambulance service. He even had a view on Master's religious attitude, which I considered was an amazing thing: that there could be other authority than the Master's (who was, in my eyes, a kind of representative of God. Of whom he preached, fervently).

Yet one late afternoon, Albert and I, it seemed, were the only people active about the Home; we were together in the top floor bathroom. He was already naked and stepping into the bath.

'We'll have a bath together,' he stated. I felt quite okay about that, even though it was unusual to have

66

a bath for us children in the afternoon, as bedtime was our bath time.

I got undressed and gingerly stepped into the water; it was not too hot, but very warm on my body. Albert was heavyset, like a man.

'Go on, sit in the water.' I followed his direction and quickly got used to the heat.

I stared at his long dick; it stuck up above the shallow water, pointing at me. It looked like a rocket. It had resonance with me: it was a powerful object.

'Touch it,' he said, his hand moving between his legs.

'Isn't it wrong?' I asked quietly. My reply was automatically repeating the instructions of my religious upbringing, which barricaded sexual matters away to an area of badness; of sin.

Albert did not blush, he was not taken aback. He was quiet for a moment, looking intently at my face. 'That's right,' he said in a matter-of-fact tone. Then silence descended. His silence puzzled me, and we soon got out of the bath – I following his example. 'Dry yourself and put on your clothes,' he told me, 'and go back downstairs.'

He left the bathroom before I had dressed, partly because I spent time standing, looking at his muscular body, the handsomeness of his long dick with its surround of hair; then watching him drying himself; and partly because I did everything in a slow fashion, all in keeping with my self-absorption and of viewing the activity around me as an observer, rather than, as the other children, a lively participator in the community.

So much for Albert – he shook down the last section of the adult's world of respectability for me. I viewed him more cautiously thenceforth, my opened mind not so believing when he spoke of "goodness" and the Bible. Master preached the body was the temple, that God created the heaven and the earth and that it was good. I still believed in Master's god, and nature was safe for me: the silence and security of the pine needle floor of the lower woods, the sweet song of a thrush there by the hedgerow, the startling beauty of a flower... and the bees everywhere upon them. I could be absorbed in the all-enclosing pleasure about me.

It was to the pine wood that I wandered on a summer's hot day: I liked the smell of the dry, crumpled wood of the derelict pavilion. It was open on three sides, to the disused asphalt-covered tennis courts, the mesh wire fence surround still in good order, but the gate facing the driveway rusty and locked. I got in by the gap at the hut's side, where previous users had pushed away the mesh fencing to make a small entry, big enough for the likes of me and other boys. I sat on its narrow bench and daydreamed of the boys and adults playing tennis there – a thing I had never seen. Now the courts had small clumps of dandelion plants growing up here and there; and in the corners, piles of windswept pine needles and small sticks; the haunt of insects of all sorts and the ground-domain of ants. White butterflies and comma butterflies flew around the straggly lilac blooms and settled on the warm wood planks, some faintly lifting off to the air, which held the familiar smell of creosote, long since painted dark and sunk in to a pale grey. This place became a hideaway of privacy for me. As was the upper driveway Cedar of Lebanon tree, whose broad branches held me as I lay there on my back, gazing up to the high windows of the house. I was hidden but I could see the house and any person who looked out of a window. But it was rare I saw anyone, the Saturday afternoons being times of absence from general routine activity. In these places of privacy I could be as one with nature; in such security I felt safe and happy.

I recall that I was a gentle, "passive" boy (often used by other boys as an American Indian, caught, and tied to a post in the field, surrounded by a crowd of cowboys yelling at me. I didn't mind this play – my position in the game felt natural to me, and eventually I would be released when the cowboys got fed up with their game). Robert responded to my quiet way, as if to try to jerk me into life. In the Home's cellar one afternoon he held me by my throat and slowly squeezed it, tighter and tighter. I seemed not to mind, but dispassionately, I thought, that I had better respond, because it might kill me, and so I struggled a little and he let my neck free. Similar behaviour by Robert, of "testing" my aliveness, happened on one afternoon in the town's swimming pool, where we went regularly each Saturday.

(I liked swimming a lot. I was in my own world under the water; my life here under my own control; and afterwards, the buying and eating of black pudding, from the nearby butcher's shop, was a regular pleasure, especially in the cold weather.)

This particular swim-day Robert held me underwater (he was stronger by age and muscular and I had no chance to wrestle free from his hold). However, I thought I would behave like the tiddler fish I had seen survive in the local streams, seemingly playing dead when under threat. I struggled really hard for a couple of seconds (saving time and air enough to last out my plan) then I let myself go totally limp – this, with the idea to fool him in thinking he had drowned me. It worked out: he let go of his grip on me. And, like the tiddler, I immediately darted off, swimming deep in the water and away to the poolside, soon bursting up through the water for air; he didn't swim after me but left me by myself. We were close friends, but one afternoon I teased him on the play of his surname and called him 'Plum', but he did not like this and told me to stop, but I kept on saying it: 'Plum, Plum.'

'I'll hit you if you keep saying that,' he told me. But I was stuck in this challenge without reason, or control, of my behaviour, and repeated the name-calling. He punched me on my arm and I cried and through my tears I kept repeating, quieter and more quiet, the word 'plum', till I finally stopped as my tears took over my emotions. We were still brotherly friends, even after this episode.

Yet Robert showed me the world about us. Which
wild vegetation to eat: young hawthorn leaves; and
the sour sorrel leaf, to chew in springtime. What plant
to dig deep under, to its pignut root, for food; and to
choose the new-growing acorns, to nibble on. He also
showed me the mystery of having a flame alight on
my thumb, like a candle, by lighting lighter fuel on it
– till it got too hot as the fuel was burnt up, and I had
to blow the flame out quickly. This little marvel was
revealed to me in the safety of the primary school
washroom, away from the staff, its vacant stone-
floored space not often visited by adults.

Robert, as well as being a mentor into the
workings of things, also helped me rediscover joy;
returning home from Crosscrake School he would
hold my hand and run fast down the lane, so fast my
legs could scarcely keep up with his – resulting in my
laughter, containing within it the fear of falling over,
in the speed. Within the Home's grounds he also
brought laughter to my lips, when we played on the
rope swing, tied high on our play-tree bough. He
stretched me as I hung on, clasping the thick rope,
my body height far from the sloping ground. I
laughed, shouting out, 'Don't, don't; I can't hold on!'
More laughter, and now an urge to pee; I was
stretched to my limits. He pulled still, holding onto
my ankles; my arms could take the strain no longer.
'I'm going to fall!' I called, between my gasps of
laughter. He released his tight hold, just as my mind
pictured myself crashing, face-first, down into the

sun-hardened earth. On the swing-back of the rope, with me weighted at its end, I neared the ground. I let myself fall down to safety, rolling on the play-worn slope.

I always tried to maintain my decorum of behaviour, and this situation had pushed my attempt to its extreme – with the danger of the fall and probable disaster. I got up, tired, unsure of myself, on displaying so much expression, though forced out of me. Yet I had enjoyed this exciting and sensual experience; I smiled at my play-friend.

In the primary school, the older girls took advantage of my gentle ways: they would lift me up and carry me to the outdoor rubbish heap and dump me on it, the leaves and grass cuttings cushioning my fall, and there I would lay for the time it took for them to leave me, before getting up, dusting myself down and dawdling away, outside of their play group. This behaviour, treating me as a toy-thing, puzzled me – and the fact that they were girls. I had understood that boys were more powerful, over them.

With the square dancing I came to life. I enjoyed this bustle of activity and joining in with the other children in the school yard. Mr Brady, a wizened and bearded small man, with an unusual accent, would dance around like an aged pixie in his braid suit and thick, knee-length stockings, as he taught us the movement of the dances. We skipped across in a pattern of diagonals and squares, merrily dancing here and there to the sound of a wind-up gramophone – and all in the open air. We laughed as we danced: boys and girls together.

My Barrows Green Home's report stated, in my tenth year of age:

Eric has made satisfactory progress since last report. He seems to be taking life a little more seriously than before. Not suitable for boarding-out.

By now, Head Office, in London, was reviewing my "special attention" status, after a previous year of assessing that, "He needs much rest, being of that highly strung vivacious type". The message now to the authorities was, "I think we could say that Eric now approximates closely a normal boy of his age, but highly strung".

Head Office replied, "Appears no reason why this Department should watch boy specially".

9

GOOD TIMES AND NEW EXPERIENCES

Habits: Good. Occasional nocturnal enuresis.
Hobbies: Reading. Stamp collecting.

Here, at Barrows Green, I had self-responsibility
thrust on me; I was approaching nine years of age.
At times, I imagined myself high-spirited and in
laughter: Mr Savidge's annual report noted:

Eric is a lively, happy lad with a keen sense of
humour. His hobbies are reading and stamp
collecting.

Yet at many times I saw myself in sorrow – perplexed
at the adults' expectation of me, and their behaviour
toward me. Even Mr Savidge would shout at times,
and stomp about giving dictates on how the Home
should be run, to the staff and his wife (often the two
of them also arguing over a particular course of
action toward a child). Because of this conflict, life
was frightening and noisy often, from the adults.
Added to this confusion, I could not understand why
I *should* have to eat my rice pudding if I didn't like

milk; and why *should* I have to go out to the field "to play" when all *I* wanted was to sit quietly in the playroom, looking at books, or daydream, staring out of the latticed windows? I never saw the Master's son being directed in such a manner: he had free range to do as he pleased in his life (and because of this, I was envious of him).

Not that all life was a mental torture of confusion at Barrows Green; there were good times, especially since Mr Clarke left, and Mr Savidge arrived in his place. The new Master was married and had a son my age. Luckily the son, Andrew, and I palled up – least till the difference of opportunity revealed itself in schooling choice: he went to grammar school, I did not. And he had two parents with him, and their support.

That being stated – he and all the orphanage children took part in the Home's social life: we had our holidays on Walney Island, camping down in a term-vacated elementary school.

It was on this island where I saw my first albino bird, a sand martin, swerving its way, low, over the sand hills. And there, of an evening, I watched the startling glory of a gold and crimson sun set as it sank slowly over the swaying Irish sea; and nightly, as I watched, silent and by myself in the moonlight, leaning against the row of black metal classroom coat stands, the display of the local furnace slag of the ship-building works, silvery shining in the dark, as it slipped down the waste heap, toward the Barrow-in-Furness estuary.

In the daytime, the fun of running with a car tyre casing: whacking, then guiding it with a short stick to keep it moving, this activity being on the expanse of the elementary school playground, the whole school empty for our holiday use. At night we slept on the assembly hall's parquet floor.

On this holiday I had my first feel of being an individual: I wandered, one afternoon, from the empty hall, into a side-room. There Andrew's granddad sat, playing cards. Vertical lines of playing cards lay on a small table before him. This sight, of cards being used in the family surprised me; had not Master often spoke of the wrong of gambling – cards and drink? I thought that this display of cards would not be allowed. But it was Granddad, and I knew, from previous times when he had argued, heatedly, with Master about some issue (for I had seen them when wandering by the office porch) that Granddad was a person of his own importance.

'This is a game of Patience,' Granddad told me, seeing me stare at what he was doing: placing cards one on top of the other, extending the columns. I liked the pictures of King and Queen and the mysterious Jack; it was all a forbidden world which teased my curiosity. I stood by his chair for some time, even to the point when he stopped playing, got out his penknife and cut up an apple, its red skin shiny. I watched him eat the white, moist slices; my mouth watering to bite on them also.

'You should be out playing in the yard. Don't you

like sunshine?' he asked me, stopping his little activity as he spoke.

'Yes,' I replied quickly and pictured the outside yard. I stood a few moments longer then thought to leave. The sensation being there was fulfilling: Granddad had spoken to me as a person; I was not just one of the children. I was happy about this personal discovery, and glad that I had dared to wander into his room and private cards game.

It was on this holiday that Peter teased me one afternoon as we sunbathed on the dusty-grey asphalt playground: 'What would you do if a girl without clothes on walked by?'

I was flummoxed at his question, as I imagined a naked girl as best I could, but no thoughts came into my head to reply. Albert, nearby also sunbathing, spoke up: 'You shouldn't be saying such things to Eric.' I felt awkward at this intrusion, but said nothing. Peter said, 'Oh, it's just a bit of fun.' After this we all continued our sunbathing in silence.

Walking across the bridge, coming back to Walney Island from a visit to Barrow Library, passing by the huge crowd of shipyard workers, all in their dark-blue dungaree-style uniforms, another older boy asked me: 'Do you know where babies come from?'

A vision popped into my mind of high white-tiled walls in a small, claustrophobic alcove, and in the background a mother carrying a wrapped-up baby in a bundle of white crochet coverings: 'They get them from hospitals,' I said, looking up to him, feeling that my knowledge was obvious. He smiled and stared at me, but said nothing more, and I silently walked beside him, a bit puzzled at his lack of response, with the white-tiled hospital walls still pictured in my mind.

One day a local girl from Walney – she was friendly, smiling and chatty – took a small group of us for a walk. To be with a totally different woman – seeming to be only about the age of our Home's most senior boy, and giving us her happiness – was a sunny surprise. She was natural and at ease in our company, as we were in hers. My heart sang with her presence, even though she was holding other boys' hands, and not mine. I understood this, as they were younger than me, and needed her help. We skipped along with her to keep up; our chatter and the sun and the fresh estuary breeze enlivened us all, and our little group was all joy that day. Her name was Rita.

On this northwest coast we swam in the sea; it was either here in Walney or Heysham, or even Arnside, as we had days out to those seaside places. On such a trip I swam out, further and further peering ahead, wanting to reach the horizon; it was a focus for me, and I kept on going. Not many minutes later I heard, very distant behind me, the calling of Master; I turned my head, and saw him waving: a small figure in the distance, beckoning for me to return to the beach. It was a shock to see how far I had swum; I got a little frightened, suddenly realising that

I was way out and alone, the other swimmers were specks near the beach-line. I looked about me to the vast expanse of sea. I thought then, to return to land, a little regretful that my voyage to that distant goal had to be given up. On my way back I tried to feel how far the seabed was under me. Not touching its base, I momentarily panicked, but regained my composure, knowing that I must keep on swimming; and so I did, toward the beach and Master, the water becoming shallow and so enabling me, every so often, to stand, touching at last, the seabed.

Swimming so far out, I had believed that I could reach, reach something I had not pictured but felt was there for me; something better than my present unhappiness: a future without sorrow.

Like the sea-fields of green that lay at the back of the Home; over which I used to stare, copying almost, the stance of the local old farmer I sometimes saw standing, leaning on his stick, looking out, silently, over the fields; I wondered what lay over that rise of land, I tried to imagine the beyond but it was a tantalising mystery. Even as I urged my mind to picture that other world, and saw myself, travelling there, I could not realise a destination. And from the hold of the Home, I could not move away.

After summer came the autumn season's celebrations: the joyful times in the large dining area, of party games at Halloween (oranges held by chins and tucked into our neck and passed to the next child, neck to neck, without using hands, they being behind our back). And another game: we were blindfolded and told to walk between plates on the floor (after they had been taken up, unbeknown to us, the blindfolded players). Rougher, high-spirited games such as musical chairs – where music being played is stopped, then everyone has to scramble to find a place to sit on from a long line of chairs, one chair being taken away after each sitting scramble. Whoever is without a chair after the scramble is out of the game – till the winner is the only one sitting on the last, and only, chair.

Home-baked party cakes, cones of sponge covered in red jam and speckled with coconut gratings and topped with a red cherry. Delicious fairy cakes, sponge with butter cream, topped with wings of sponge. Other cakes too, but I remember these two types, and the eager moments of eating such infrequent delights.

And in the evening: placing the hollowed out pumpkin on the open side porch wall, a candle lit inside; the eyes and mouth glowing yellow into the darkness as night came on; a most mysterious appearance of a lifelike thing, to which I stared on longer in fascination, after my companions had gone back indoors. In a smaller group of older boys (and I would stay too, allowed to listen, such was my intent interest shown) Master told stories of ghosts he had seen. One, of a dark evening he had gone to the kitchen garden, and coming back from the gate he had turned back to see a tall grey ghost moving from the gate and into the nearby woods, disappearing there. He told of stuff, like white fluffy glue, coming from a person's fingers as they pulled them apart, from the arched force of them pressing together, held like a church arch, for minutes before – to enable the making of this substance. It came from the creation of the pressure, from the person's own body power.

Christmas time was a joy. In the same large dining room a giant conifer tree was fixed. It was decorated to bursting, with pink, red, and white Christmas lights; and spread around, like a showy dress, with glistening tinsel. And amongst all this splendour were tiny hanging parcels, glinting in their golden covering. The tree stood, always alight, in the alcove next to the fireplace, well away from the high marble mantelpiece, its top tip touching the ceiling.

On the Christmas day morning we were all allowed to pick up our presents: the floor was covered in brightly wrapped shapes – we tripped carefully over other boys' gifts till we found our own named parcel, all donated by the local Rotary Club and voluntary supporters, including those from the Methodist church fundraisers. A toy tractor was my most impressive gift. I would play with it for hours – by myself, and imagine driving it down the lane, where we walked to school, manoeuvring each small bend, and up the hill and down again. The wheels turned by the steering wheel so I could let it travel over my private area of floor – and dream away in pleasure – in my own world of imagination.

Toward the late afternoon, Master gave us an old gramophone to play with; it intrigued me greatly, so much so that I ended up remaining the only boy playing its one spiked metal disc. I tried to puzzle out how the tin disc, about eight inches across, with small triangular bits poking out, could make music. It did, by another piece of metal clipping on the upraised pieces as the disc moved round and round. The melody on the only disc was 'Suwanee River'; the notes clicked one at a time into the air. It was an effort to wind the gramophone up, just to hear one tune.

These hours were full of happiness: to see the pretty world of glittering coloured patterns through my kaleidoscope, subtly changing at each delicate movement of my fingers; and about me on the polished parquet floor, the glinting Christmas gold, emerald and blue of the foil-wrapped chocolates all filled my imagination with unbearable and inexpressible pleasure; the tall, lighted Christmas tree, the yellow flames of the log fire and the chatting, joyful company of my companions; for these moments I was home – they gave warmth to the small inner glow of my heart.

Winter was a wild delight; and when snow came and settled in a thick layer as it did each year, we would crowd around and onto our homemade wood sledges and crash down the near field, stopping on a level just before the danger of the barbed wire fence that separated the row of cherry trees before the hedge, at a level above the public lane winding below.

Being cold, with numb-white fingers and excited at the same time, was a peculiar mixture: pain and joy together. And going indoors, afterwards, for afternoon tea, made the house a cosy happy atmosphere like a real home, for we all were in reality a large family – albeit of twenty or so boys, and the Master's son.

Though we slept in large dormitories, five or so to a bedroom, at meal times we were all together, four boys at each little table, one boy each side – except those tables with a staff member attending – and Matron's table, where her son also sat. It was at this table that I had my meals too – and the privilege of sharing the use of the small toaster at breakfast time.

Some argument had happened, after breakfast, between me and Andrew. Master had told me off. I gave a punch on Andrew's arm – not forcefully, more in defiance. 'Why did you do that?' Master asked. I looked down, sulking. I kept quiet, not looking up at all. 'Say "sorry".' Reluctantly I did. 'You are good friends: what's happened?' Master asked.

'I don't know,' I said, confused at reacting from emotions I was not sure of.

'Get ready for school, now.' And the small gathering of other boys, that had hung about to see what was happening, dispersed quickly. In my heart I was envious of Andrew; that he was the Master's son, not me; that he had all the things I did not have, including freedom to go about the Home as he wished, without the adult control of his life that I had. He could choose; I could not. I edged away, following the other boys. I was a little surprised that Master had not been angry at my behaviour.

Andrew had the privacy of his own bedroom. Seeing it through his half-opened door, as I would pass by, presented a different world to me: his own shelf of books, his own mantle-piece of trinkets and toys, his own pictures to decorate the papered walls – a dressing table, mirrors – and a large cuddly duvet on the soft bed (Andrew did invite me in sometimes, to sit on his bed while we talked, or I'd watch as he fiddled with the ornaments in his room).

Even so, his bedroom, and its adornments, was a distant kind of life to my existence. I couldn't really grasp it. It was there, yet just out of reach: my emotions, held tight and frozen up as they were, would not allow me to regret, to desire this paradise of individuality before me. Also, it did not allow me the risk for my heart to seek back to my first home – partly imagined, as *my* own small paradise, of so long ago: with Gran, a brother and the occasional appearance of my mother, for she left for the cotton mill, early in the morning. My busy daily life at Barrows Green made me soon forget this past world.

We, the orphanage boys, had the playroom; and for me, it was a haunted place; rather it had a "presence" especially when no one was there except me, in the airy daytime, to sense its atmosphere. The room was large, its windows were low and spread across the curve of an alcove the length of one wall; it had pictures on the walls of childhood scenes: some with fairies standing in a glade surrounded by a ring of toadstools, the fairies' wings clear with the sunlight. Over the floor *Argosy* magazines, with their windblown pen drawing of a mast ship sailing away, at an angle, as if in the sky. This sailing ship picture held my imagination. Of it, I sensed there was a "somewhere", outside of my present life – though oddly, I never opened up the front cover, just daydreamed on its image. I have mixed up images of the many different magazines that piled here and there over the parquet floor like a small sea of stilled waves.

Often, partly opened books lay around the skirting boards: old, adult-style books as well as child picture books; more play things than books for reading. These adult books had hard, stiff covers. One that always took my attention had black and white pictures, almost like photographs. There was a particular picture that held my gaze often: a plump lady, naked and chained to a huge rock overhanging a raging sea of high waves, and an eagle bird, with talons spread out, speeding down at an angle toward her. She appeared to be pulling, straining on the chains, yet her effort was benign somehow; her full fleshy, Mother Earth abundance of form belied her pictured struggle. This image, with the dilemma of the lady, resonated with me, though I did not know its meaning, of the picture, or the story (which I did not attempt to read, for at this time, I "looked" at such books of cramped print, not often attempting to read them).

A "Rupert" book also held my rapt attention, by the mystery of a black-clad pixie sitting on a toadstool, and Rupert coming up to him, asking some question of direction. Later on, I found pleasure and a private existence for myself on being allowed to visit the town's library; its cosy atmosphere and carpeted floor enclosed me in safety. Joy also secured my attention: all the many books everywhere – for me to choose; it overwhelmed me. I stood still and stared, enraptured by the sight about me. I hesitated to take the two small steps up and into the "Adults" section – I was not an adult, yet that area with many more books than the children's bookshelves enticed me. I was frustrated and unhappy on the banishment to entry by that one word; what was hidden by that word? I wanted to look, to read, sure that I was able to manage; but reluctantly I backed away.

However, I found my place, and happiness, in my "Children" library section. There I read a delightful picture book, very small, about ants: their queen was all glamorous, with big eyelashes. The tale was told of her flying up into the sky and meeting a handsome male ant and "marrying" in the sky.

Much later, when probably ten years old, I enjoyed the *Famous Five* books of Enid Blyton, so much so that I joined her "Famous Five Club" and received a badge of membership. (On reflection, I am surprised that the adults bothered to fulfil my wishes as regards my reading interest in joining this club; they must have stuck on a stamp and posted the letter of application for me, after all, I wasn't the Master's son or the like.) I saw lots of "Biggles" books lying about the playroom; and maybe later on actually read a Capt. W. E. Johns-authored book.

In the summer evenings and on Saturdays, we had lots of spare time to make our "dens". They consisted of basic wood planks, as platforms, joining some of the close-growing fir trees, some tall Scots pines, in the wooded area by the drive of the Home. At least we had, it seemed, free range in climbing and playing in the trees. Similarly with walks: we, usually with the Master, had long trails around the local hillsides. I remember one particular high hill and the effort each time to reach the pointed pinnacle; of the buzzard floating higher over me, and the wind blowing through my hair. Ahead, and out of reach of the other boys, I could shout, could sing – and cry tears of joy (even so, the other children thought it was the sharp wind in my eyes) for here I was free. Also, I would dawdle, or frequently wander off, having to rush later to catch up with the walking group ahead. But all of us would climb halfway up the hill to enjoy the slide down the compact grass of climbers' pathways which ran through the high bracken; bracken taller than us. But only if the hot days made the ground dry – and we would have to watch out to miss the bits of lime rock sticking out of the hillside, though sometimes our bottoms got knocks, such would be our speed of descent, laughing the way down.

From this high hill walk, we once crossed over a main road that went through a village, called Natland. It was a proper village compared to the hamlet size of Sedgwick, through which we passed on our long walks. In Natland lay a wide green at its centre. In different directions, three or more paths marked their ways across the green, leading to other roads and to rows of cottages. Somehow a lady let me into one cottage. I was dawdling at its front garden, admiring the hollyhocks and the other flowers in full bloom. 'Come in, dear, have a look.' The lady in the garden invited me.

'Go in,' Master directed me. Inside the ceiling was low, and I asked the lady (she was not much taller than me, all wrapped in clothes and motherly in shape) what the big, rough-looking hooks in the ceiling were.

'Well dear, they were for hams to be hung up – you know, pig meat.' This reply scared me a little, but my curiosity remained, as I looked about the walls and ceiling.

'Thank you. I have to go now,' unsure what would happen to me in this small place, for I was used to large rooms and big houses, for all my Homes were such places. And feeling confined now, and with a strange adult, made me insecure.

'Yes, dear, you must go.'

And so I returned to the full light of day and the familiar crowd of boys, with Master.

On our walks to get to Levens Park, we passed

through the small street of Sedgwick village; the pavement was narrow – so close was it to the cottages that we could see in the tiny windows. There I looked upon a tall lady in a swirling shaped gown, an Alsatian dog on a lead beside her. This ornament on the window sill was light brown and shiny. I never saw anyone inside the house – or even in the one street passing through the village. There was just our small crowd and Master about, giving noise of chatter and ambling. Sometimes we walked above the level of Sedgwick, onto high ground, to reach the canal, called the Lancaster Canal. There we walked, played or ran along its narrow path. At some stage the canal had been dried out, now rushes and tall plants grew there; they flowered where once water filled the deep curve of space. Wasps were everywhere, and though we were tempted to go down into the deep grasses and growths, the wasps kept us out.

The walk through the Levens Park woods was the most exciting. Beneath the huge avenue of trees the place became a fairyland of nature: the wide slow-flowing river, ten minutes run away from the trees, showed me my first dipper bird. This little black bird, with a wide white throat, like a bib at meal times, ran through the clear water, running and darting over the pale stones on the river bed. It surprised me that a bird could do this – be underwater; but there it was, searching and prodding for food.

By the river, called the Kent, bright kingcups,

with their yellow shiny petals, stood tall. The sight of them delighted me, and increased my wonder and joy at this half-deserted place, full of nature and her sounds.

The swing bridge, high above the same river, further on, was fun. Master let us all run across it – we pushed the rope sides and made the bridge sway; yet we felt safe, although we were so high up. The wide river a long way below did leave me in awe; and with it, the echo of our chatter and laughter over its clear passageway. All this, and the avenue of huge trees, and the vast wild nature of it all, held me in wonder.

Further on from the river, herons had their noisy nesting places: a "heronry", as I later checked in my little *Observer Book of Birds*. I wondered how such big birds could make nests to settle up at the top of the trees, and who crowded together. They reminded me of the rooks and their group of nests, in the swaying tops of the trees near Oxenholme Station, where the Home's car passed by sometimes, on the side road toward Kendal; where once I dared myself to climb: up and up, in the sway of smaller branches till I reached my arm high above my head and into the cawing rooks' nest, feeling, in all my excitement, the large warm eggs. Then to carefully climb down the soot-darkened bark; my breathing quickened by the exhilaration of my completed venture, and aware all the time of the sound of the steam engines puffing out but yards away on their tracks below me; but finally, to reach the firm safety of the ground.

One time, in Levens Park, when I wandered off from the walk group, I saw a fawn, by itself. I moved slowly up near to it. It appeared to want to jump over the low metal fencing before it. The fawn knew I was near, but it could not jump high enough to escape me. I saw it was trapped between the fence and me. I took pity on the fawn's frightened stance and gently backed away to let it go free.

On another of our walks, near the fells, across the rugged area of the landscape, a car ride away from the Home, I wanted to run away – and I did – from the group. I was miserable and wanted freedom from my life. I imagined – and thought of how I would survive – by hiding under one of the overhanging rocks, and eat berries and dig up pignuts and chew on sorrel leaves and young dock leaves and crab apples and rose hips (after much care with taking out the irritable hairy seeds). But on crossing a road to reach another craggy fell-side, I encountered the Home's car. It stopped and Master called me over: 'Come on, get in. I've been looking all over for you!' And so, sulkily, I had to re-enter the Home's control. I got in the car without much ado and we all drove on back to the Home, Master never knowing, or questioning me, for the intention of my absence.

10

SCHOOL AND CHURCH

Australia: "Have you any parents?"

Primary school took us down this long winding lane –
past the old farmhouse and its craggy orchard in the
front, past the slope of grassland flowing with reddish-
brown hens, the swallows swooping in and out of their
part-opened henhouse on the hill rise. On the way, our
walking sustained in summer by the flowing roadside
stream – the cool water refreshing us, and its watercress
giving us boys a peppery chew. Up the hill we regularly
made our passage, past the shady bank where the
mysterious cuckoo pint grew, displaying its stiff stem
of clustered orange berries, half cloaked around with
fine, protective leaf; then over the rise before the steep
rundown to the crossroads, and further down, after a
five minute stroll, the low grey-stone school.

On these daily trips, about a mile long, I used to
dawdle, and so often, just by myself, watch the
swallows skimming over the hedges and the fields; I
would be discovering, at the level of my head, the
secret sitting robin on its nest, hidden in the mossy
hedge bank, its beady brown eyes unblinking as my
eyes peered into its face; and experiencing the shock
of sudden blue of a single egg in a hedge sparrow's

nest; and looking up at the high hedgerow and its pink-petalled dog roses, and making up in my head little couplets of rhyme, about the sky, the birds and their sweet singing, even as I watched the flitting of yellowhammers onto the hedge-top twigs.

And in the late summer, stopping on my walk to listen to the exited twittering of the swallows, sitting in line along the telegraph wires, ready for their long journey across the land and seas. If I lost my play marble, with its pretty swirls of blue and green, after wobbling it precariously over the worn lane, I would pray to God, 'please, please let me find it,' my clasped fingers hurting in my anguish. But I still, eventually, had to open my eyes, and in great hope, search in the tall grasses of the verge. So determined was I to seek it out, that I would keep looking till I found it, forgetting about school for, traipsing toward there alone, I would again be late.

Along the lane, and on the further hillside top, the wide verge near a field gate was sometimes occupied by a ragged tramp, his face leathery and brown from the sun. He was well wrapped in sack-like coats and had a straggly brown beard. His eyes were shiny and wild. Passing by him, very cautiously, being by myself sometimes, I would stare at his face. He frightened me but held my curiosity. I felt some empathy toward him and wanted to ask: 'What's in your big sack?' but I dare not stop to speak, thinking that I may end up in that bound sack. I imagined he kept stolen hens in there.

A tramp, similar to the lane one, called one day at the back door by the kitchen of the Home. I heard Master shout at him: 'It is written in the Bible that a man should eat by the sweat of his brow.' I was sad that Master refused to give the tramp any food, for which he was asking. But that was how Master was: at times preaching, when in church, and when in the Home, rushing down the corridors, giving out some instructions, to boys or staff. At other times, singing a verse of a popular hymn as he went about the Home's business; his tall image taut and tense like a biblical prophet, as I imagined one such would be.

Though of grey stone, the school building inside appeared of all wood; the floors were dusty planks and the desks hard, polished wood. There were high, tall windows on all sides (except where the narrow stove stood, surrounded by a metal railing, where rows of small milk bottles were placed in winter to warm up before we drank them). The headmaster's desk was large, with a big blotter pad, some papers, pens, and his tobacco pipe stand. Mr Johnstone was a serious-looking man – and I wondered at him, why he never seemed to smile or chatter, like us. He was slow and solid, and silent most of the time. He never shouted or seemed cross, but was considerate, if slightly stern in appearance. One day, in 1952 I think, he could not get the radio Home Service on: it was silent – then later we heard the news that the king, George VI, had died. There may have been solemn music playing, but Mr Johnstone was especially sombre that day. Though I could not understand the full import of "death of the king", I knew it must have been very serious... but the following year there was celebration, with a school party, as a new queen was being made in a "coronation". Unhappily I missed the trestle table party as I moved to attend school in the town. From the activity at the local village green I knew that the seating forms at the school would be put out in the playground, and the coloured red, white and blue triangular bunting displayed under the eaves of the school house, and the children, without me, would be seated joyfully, eating cakes and sandwiches and drinking orange juice, and eating ice cream and yellow and green jelly. But I would feel old anyway, for that school now, I was in the big school, the secondary modern, and my boundary of life would grow bigger – even as I seemed to shrink into myself.

Maths tables, which we recited by heart at primary school, intrigued me: I couldn't work out how 7 x 7 could make 49 – the 9 ending didn't figure for me as being right. So it was, by this seeming oddity, that I always remembered that particular multiplication line: 7 x 7 = 49. The twelve times maths table also intrigued me (the word "twelve" seemed unusual – a strange word which stood out in my mind). That twelve could go up, in multiplication, to such a high number, past one hundred, excited me. It also appeared neat to be able to cut up number twelve by twos (and six fitted tight into twelve, which made me happy).

But in my primary school, I loved to sit, silent and awe-bound like the other children, when Miss Earnshaw or Mr Birkett, a gentle man with a big, bushy moustache, read out a story. These lessons were the best times at school, and I could not understand why we could not sit there for all the day hours, listening to stories. Another woman teacher read stories also; her name always slipped my mind yet she fascinated me. Her face was very sun-tanned, sallow really. I was comfortable in her presence; I had a warm attraction toward her in my heart. She sat, large as certainty itself, reading tales to the still and silent class. But break times came and play, or going to the toilets in the far end of the yard, into the smelly dark-brown tin buckets which reminded me of the local farm cow stall, where we went to collect the Home's small churn of milk, once or twice a week – though the toilet smell was a mixture of creosote and something else. But I did not mind this backend area of the school, as it was usually unpopulated with other children, or school teachers, and their absence gave me a sense of myself and gave the peace of the surrounding pasture fields.

One day, I must have asked to be excused from lesson to go to the toilet, for I was there alone. My heart beat fast at my sudden freedom. I had in me a need to be naked, and to climb the high, dry-stone wall that separated the school grounds from the surrounding field. I managed to get up, and wanted to feel the sun-hot stone on my bottom, but with my shorts down my legs to my ankles, I slipped from the wall top and brought down a large stone slab, entangled in my shorts. I was cut with a deep gash under my ankle, and it bled. I didn't seem to feel any pain and went back into the classroom, my sock covering the gash, but one of the boys saw all the blood; and I think I must have looked paler than my usual pale complexion, for suddenly all attention was on me. The teacher directed a boy to take me back home (after myself protesting feebly that I was 'all right'). Turning around in my seat, I saw that that boy was Robert: he carried me by piggyback – he was like a big brother to me, and strong, yet he had to stop every now and again to rest, to put me down a few moments; and so we made our way to the Home's door.

I explained to Master that I fell off the wall at school. The Doctor was called and he stitched the gash up – and (as usual with me, and different from most of the other boys), I did not cry at all, did not know how, for my emotion, I was discovering more often, was frozen inside of me. I just stared at the stitching procedure and at the cold flap of flesh, as I sat very still on the medical room stool. The stitches were taken out a week or so later and I soon returned to my routine of life in the Home, forgetting the wall experiment that sunny day, and the hot exciting sting of stone on my naked bottom.

The adult I mainly looked up to was Master, Andrew's father. I admired him. In his preaching, he stood up boldly in the Sunday morning pulpit and openly gave his messages of the Bible, and enthusiastically sang the Christian songs. I guess, deep down, he was my true image of a grown-up; his words and his daily behaviour at least had a resonance with me and my religious sentiment – for Jesus was meek and mild, though Master, at times, was as loud and fierce as any prophet proclaiming forth; he had no compunction over the necessity of life. (He shocked me one cold afternoon when, on finding a baby mouse in his sitting room, took it outside on to the stone tiles of the open porch, and stamped his foot on it. I stood, stunned, in silence. Similarly, I watched him wring the necks of hens, to kill for the kitchen. I helped with the plucking of their feathers, the finer ones aggravating me by sticking onto my sweaty face.)

So I was instructed, by example, that killing, death, was a needful, natural, happening of life. It was a hard wall of fact I could not get over, like the limitation of thought which Mr Clarke had forced on me, barely two years earlier, when he had pictured to me through his words, the image of my crucifixion. Of both, I had to accept – could not escape – their raw realities.

I strove to be like Jesus; it fitted in with my oppressed emotional life, I suppose – being humble was an achievable goal for me, for I had no possessions, no privacy. I was a vessel, empty for the service of others.

Sunday school at the Home, in the hut near the apple orchard, was taken by Master, Mr Savidge, telling us stories from the Bible, in his own words, as we sat enthralled all around him on the hard composite floor; of God speaking to Moses from the burning bush; of the fearless vivid appearance of Daniel in the lion's den, his long hair like the lion's head; the regular saying of the Lord's Prayer. The image of a benign but solemn, white-bearded father figure, not unlike Mr Johnstone from the primary school, in solemnity, but without the godly beard, rested on puff-white clouds of glory, slowly sailing in the heavens; like the same clouds that gathered over my head in the vision I had at the day convention I later attended: "to come to Jesus and be saved". "Our Father, which chart in Heaven…" and I pictured a worn, dust-covered sea map, like a pirate treasure map with a wind-filled sailing ship moving over it… "Hallowed be they name… Thy kingdom come…" and the vastness of the fields, hills and countryside filled my mind till, "Thy will be done…" my hold then would be lost, mixing a nascent guilt with judgement of the small wrongdoings of the moment, or of recent days – and "forgiveness" weighed heavy in my breast: that *I* should be "forgiven" for the thing I felt, but could not voice, or figure in my mind; then the calm that came over me: "Give us our daily bread… forgive them that trespass against us… deliver us from evil… Thine is the Kingdom… forever and ever. Amen."

It was Master who had the most influence on me. His biblical stories emphasised, to me, the value of one's time on earth: temporal; that each life should be used and spent wisely and to the common good; that one should not waste the hours of the day, in idleness. The lesson of the three talents: to use our gifts wisely, not to bury away or waste our worth. He retold the parables of the Bible and interpreted the stories, mainly of the Old Testament, for our eager ears and hearts: David standing up to Goliath; the Good Samaritan, whose kindness touched my heart; the mystery of Jacob's ladder, leading up into the clouds; the Wise Virgins, waiting, standing in line, a story which I could not understand, but the imagery of their lighted lamps and, as I imagined, their hooded and blue-draped forms, filled my mind.

Language and stories were the food of my imagination on Sundays, and that day was a weekly day of sustenance and peace: a stillness that lasted for the whole day, which I always looked forward to, again. Some evenings I had a small gathering of younger children around me as they listened to little stories I told them. There were bits of Master's tales and bits of my made-up tales. I pictured them as I told them, lived them at the moment of telling. My added pieces were of exploration – in caves and secret trapdoors. What I knew from Master's stories mixed in my imagination, coming out as by themselves, into little tales. Then I would suddenly stop, as if my treasure chest of stories had emptied out. Master reminded me of my storytelling activity before I left Barrows Green, a few years later, as I was not that aware of this behaviour of mine at the time.

Sunday was also the day for the long walks, Master being our usual leader. It was like, as I now visualise, the shepherd leading his flock; and we browsed, as it were, stopping to wander or play, then he would call us on, leading us out and back home, safely again. It was a sense of personal freedom which, like other activities, I received from these walks; it was my private, inner self with nature, in closeness to the air which gave me a powerful sense of my being, an affirmation which gave me happiness. One such walk showed my inner tenacity – or my tightly held stunted emotional condition. It had rained and it was winter time, all of us children came back soaked, very cold and howling in tears. All, that was, except me. I did not cry but stoically presented myself, like the other drowned rats of childhood, to the waiting staff.

My fingers were stiff and white with the cold: 'Eric, go into the kitchen; you are a brave boy, not crying. Put your hands in warm water.' And I was left to myself. I felt that I was special, grown-up in some inner way, compared to my peers; physical hurt did not affect me, it was almost a separate place to me, to my inner, *real* self. And I had been taught that our body is but a covering for the "inner temple", the more sacred self. I needed the peace of nature and the spiritual respite of Sunday.

I was known as 'Eggy'; I was always on edge; a tinderbox of sensitivity. At the least little occasion of interference, or contact by another boy, and I would react in a temper. I don't know why; I was a frightened child, I suppose, and any approach was a threat, or a disturbance, to my peace, for I kept to my own company most of the time. Yet I had one or two friends whom I kept very close too. They were very "male-like" compared to my gentle nature; that, I think, was the attraction, on my part; it must have been a natural, mutual attraction, and certainly an unconscious one. There was Robert whom I followed through to my next Home, partly to be still with him, and there was Michael, a curly red-haired boy, freckled face and mischievous. We made treetop dens, climbing together, and in adventure and play we were inseparable. Paul, a curly-haired Brazilian-looking boy, had left my life some years ago. He had migrated, with Barnardo's, to Australia. I wanted to go too – I pictured that long sea voyage and sunshine – and to be with him, for I clung to him, in our friendship, though we were only about eight years of age.

'Have you any parents?' The doctor asked me, as I stood, potbellied and naked before him, as he examined me from the Master's sitting room couch. I could not think of any, then the feeling of Gran came to me, and I blurted out: 'My Gran.' And that seemed to be the decision-making moment for the doctor, and the Home: I would not be going to

Australia. I had lost Paul; and that sunshine voyage to freedom, as I imagined it. Such loss together shrank the ice of my already frozen heart – my ability to show emotion compressed into an even smaller space.

Still little in age, I was allowed to go to the village church not far from the primary school. It was Church of England (C of E), as that was my registered faith written down on entering the Homes. I was old enough, about eight or nine, and skinny enough to slip through the narrow gap beside the church organ and the wall. I had the duty on morning service to pump, by a long wooden handle jutting out from a slit in the organ side, to give air to the church music, as the organist played. Being curious and of a tendency to test little boundaries in my daily life, such as climbing very high, narrow-topped trees to find out the limits of my fear, or of entering dark places of the Home at night to test the control of my imagination of things I thought were waiting there; here in church I attempted my dare, and stopped pumping the organ. I would listen for the slow wind down of the notes before quickly pumping the music back up to full strength. This action gave me a thrill; that I had the power to control such an important situation as the music to the church – and this little trick of mine probably influenced the release of me from this duty, and quite soon too after being given it to perform. The church organ was a mystery in any case, to me. I could not fathom out how the large and thick fingers of the organist, pressed down on the keys, could make such melody. They did not bend or fiddle around on the keys like they had magic life, and did not look sensitive enough to make music – but they did of course, make the loud and sonorous sounds into the little stone church each Sunday morning, with my intermittent help.

I attended the evening service there, when allowed – and took this as a treat, such was the solemn delight of the *Nunc Dimittis* and the parting words, "Go in peace"; they gave me my inner nourishment. I would leave the church with sadness, a melancholy which satisfied my soul: such was my "spiritual" tendency at this age.

Though the gold, purple and cream-robed preacher, with grey hair and ruddy cheeks, spoke his sermon with verbal relish, I could not understand it: the jewels of his words spilled from his mouth – he sounded melodious and grand, but apart from the music of language, I could not fathom what he *meant* for most of his preaching, except the passages of the Bible which held a picture in their language, to enter my imagination and my simple understanding.

What held my imagination also was the small, plump lady, her throat and shoulders muffled in furs. When she sang her voice was louder than all others and rode over the top of the hymn being sung. Her melody was her own rhythm, out of step and beat of the rest of the congregation. I found this peculiar:

why did no one ever tell her and stop her? For, at each morning service she was the same: there she was, like a plump wren, but of dark-blue feather, puffed up, bursting out with her own particular pitch and all with unselfconscious aplomb.

After morning service we could make our own way from church, up the same long lane as to the primary school, back to the Home, careful not to step on the grassy mounds of the old graves. I would be conscious in my mind of an image of a person lying there, in their private place, quietly. Past these graves we would run up and over the burial ground to the dry-stone wall, climb over it, and from this short cut continue our homeward trek.

On one of the last visits to the C of E church, in the late autumn, returning after service, back to the Home, we giggled in excitement on the total blackness of the night: we couldn't even see our hands before our faces. We were a small group busying ourselves, like chickens round a parent bird, exploring the area before us, quickly returning to the long legs of Master, whose presence protected us. A huge dark thing scurried across our path: 'Look at that giant leaf!' someone shouted out. We hurried after it, keen to stop it moving. It was a hedgehog – and that was an exciting discovery. We let it into the depths of the roadside verge, quickly returning to Master, and our way home.

Occasionally, on a Sunday evening, I would go with Master on his lay preaching day, to hear him from the Methodist church in the local town. Sometimes, to travel with him to a mid-morning service, further away from the Home, at a more distant chapel, over the hills of Westmorland. I would seek earnestly to enter his fervour and eye-shine sincerity as he gave out his sermons. Therein was some lighting of truth – some little concern of life which connected with my needs – for I had lost, and was searching for, a return, or a reaching forth, to a fuller awareness… of what, I did not really know. His preaching – especially at the evening service – brought tranquillity to my mind – and gave solemnity to my heart. Maybe, I would be a preacher like Master, and stand tall in the pulpit, and talk and sing, and all the people would look at me and listen, held and enthralled. They would not clap, but my heart would beat like a hundred hands joining in happiness at my presence, above them, in their church.

He was a Methodist, and he asked me if I would like to join the Methodist congregation each Sunday. I said 'Yes.' I liked the new atmosphere, though at first I was surprised at the plain walls and lack of decorative beauty, but the sermons were a revelation. I could understand the meaning of what the preacher said, in the main – they were in everyday speech, and from then on, I began to consciously learn from the sermons. They were a guide to behaviour and a food to my spirit. Otherwise, I remained a solitary youngster.

From my attentiveness at church, and apparent interest in "spiritual" matters, Master arranged for me to attend, one weekend, a Bible study session at Capernwray Hall, near Carnforth, in the Cumbrian hills. This was a very inner-still time for me, and a time of changes sensed, for my primary school days would be ending soon.

At this Christian study centre I was a serious-faced boy amongst young adults, and I felt my presence integral here. Though I did not understand or see further than the spoken and written Biblical word, I felt the serenity of the gathering: the Bible study theme was "action" in the active Gospel of Luke (I was told).

About this time, during a half-day convention, I saw the vision above my head of puff-white clouds and angelic faces, even as the words of the evangelist were coming over to me: "Open the door of your heart to Jesus: let him in, now!" It was a deeper conversion, converted as I was already in the Christian Faith.

During the break times, I wandered into the hall, to the display table. There I gazed at the small neat books: John Bunyan's tales and small prayer books, laid out for sale, all bound in leather. I did not have money to buy but I ached for them, and even thought to steal one. I stood there for many seconds debating within myself if I should, but decided not to. I walked away empty-handed, but with a clear conscience.

At Capernwray I entered a new society: one of refinement and a softer gathering of people; evening dinner, formal layout of tableware, and the company of people from Germany, amongst other nationalities. I was struck, and curious, as to why the German young men did not laugh out loud as the other diners did, including myself, at the dinner speaker's humour, nevertheless I was impressed with their solid demeanour and polite ways. It was a world which took up my mind and intelligence; I was at ease here. During a free afternoon from study I enjoyed the company of a woman who was from Suffolk. She had an accent I had never heard before (no doubt she had never heard mine, from Westmorland, but I did not reflect, in my youth and innocence, on this factor). I laughed each time she spoke in our conversation, as she sounded as if her words were said in a part-joking fashion. She told me, no, it was only her accent and she was serious when she spoke, and we continued our walk down the slope of the open fields. I had my first horse ride, on my own: 'Whatever you do don't let her bend her head down to eat the verge grass; you'll never get her up again to carry on walking.' But my curiosity eventually got the better of me, and I let her lower her head to chew on the roadside grass – it looked so rich and luscious, I let her eat, I was confident and certain I could get her back again. But it was very difficult, and the man who had saddled the huge carthorse was right; I was relieved when she raised her head eventually, and responded to my urging to plod on ahead, down the lane. I felt proud and majestic so high up in the air, riding this large animal, and this image of seeing my own self vaguely reverberated in my imagination and joined the image of the farmer's daughter, of Crosscrake school days, high on her grey horse: of her silent, confident loveliness.

It was here at Capernwray also, one night, that I had my first visit of a monk-like figure, and it frightened me stiff. It stood at the end of my bed, and kept there in the quietness of the moonlit night, even though other sleepers were in the large dormitory. I closed my eyes but it was still there, minutes after I re-opened them, standing, hooded, and still; darkness filled the place where a face should have been. Though my limbs ached in stiffness, I must have fallen asleep; the daylight brought me security and certainty, yet I felt precarious in my sensibility to the atmosphere of the large mansion building, and its tall windows that glinted and shadowed into the shaded surrounding trees.

Another dark evening and another atmosphere of fear at Capernwray came about. We all gathered in the main prayer room. We sat silent and expectant at what was going to be announced. There was a tension in the air of the night-drawn curtained room. Someone, the religious leader told us, was prowling outside. This sent a wave of fear – I felt it, and stiffened where I sat. 'Let us gather together, join our hands, and pray.' Sensitively and with delicate reaching out, we held each other's hands. The outside force was spoken of as if the devil was prowling about in the dark and we, protected by the Word of the Bible, were the holy ones of God, huddled in the light of his Word, protected too by the rock-steady building of the hall. But behind me, behind the long thick drapes, I sensed the presence of evil pressing its face on the latticed glass – and in a moment of stillness my soul quivered.

'Defend us, O Lord, from the darkness without…' the leader spoke, and I let the words sink into me as I seemed to pass away from the consciousness of the room and the people about me. And suddenly, as by a miracle, the room appeared brighter, and the meeting continued, as planned, in the studying of the Gospel of St. Luke. A little frightened still, I followed the proceedings, keeping near to the safety of adult bodies sitting by me.

My second seeing of this image would be several years later – but now, I am still in the North of England.

11

SUMMER HOLIDAY
WHERE I WAS BORN

Letter from Head Office to Home: It is in order for boy to spend a holiday with his mother at 34 Water Street, Ribchester, Near Preston, Lancashire.

During one summer holiday I was allowed to go home, to my mother, in Ribchester.

> *Head Office:* Letter from Mr Savidge stating request received from mother asking for Eric to go home for a holiday from 5th to 26th August. He has agreed to let him go.

> Letter from Head Office to Home: It is in order for boy to spend a holiday with his mother at 34 Water Street, Ribchester, Near Preston, Lancashire.

The cottage, in Water Street, was small, especially after the roomy spaces of Barrows Green. But surrounding the village were fields and a wide river, the Ribble. The next-door boy, Frank, being about my age, came with me on adventure outings over the fields. I would test his skills at jumping over gullies

in the land and over small waterways. I was
surprised that beating me was not important to him;
I was much more competitive. But he had only
maybe a few local lads to compete with in play,
whereas I had a crowd of boys, eager to survive, and
the open environment to be tested in.

I liked Frank, he was relaxed and friendly. His
mother I liked also. She looked like a gypsy: very
dark hair and black eyes. She was shorter than me,
even at my age of about twelve then. Her eyes
appeared always to be laughing; she was chatty and
helped out my mother with various foodstuffs when
my mum was short of things. Frank's dad was very
quiet and gentle and very tall; he only said 'Hello',
and such things to me; anyhow, I did not really see
much of him – out at work, I guess.

Running out of bread one afternoon, my mother
asked me to call over the road. Just opposite our
door, number 34, was a cottage, really a small hut.
Within it was a small, grocer type shop. I had to step
down from the road to get to the doorway, as the
shop hut was at a lower level to the other buildings
there, facing the road.

'Yes, luv, what can I get for you?'

'A loaf of bread please, for my mum.'

'Oh, are you from across the road? I haven't seen
you before.'

'Yes,' I innocently, and eagerly, replied. 'I'm
visiting on holiday.'

'Never knew she had another one there; or

maybe I'd forgotten,' she mused to herself, more than talking to me.

I could not quite understand her meaning. Not till years later my unease from that meeting was realised: she only remembered my brother's existence, not another child having been born to Mum. However, a bit puzzled by her preoccupation and sudden lack of attention at my departing, with the bought bread, I left her shop, and forgot about her, on entering Mum's front door.

Back inside the cottage, I enjoyed Gran's black-gloss rocking chair, testing its stability on how far it would go back without toppling over: this when Gran was out of the living room; I, generally feeling, the head of the home.

In the living room, fixed into one wall, was the black, cast-iron range with its coal fire for cooking, and side compartments for keeping things warm, including the earthenware hot water bottles at night-time. There was also a small cooker in the back kitchen, but it did not seem to be on much of the time.

It was in the back kitchen, at the large chipped stone sink, that all the washing of stuff was done: clothes and pots. I washed myself there, too, standing before it. A small set of window panes looked out onto the garden from over the deep, square basin. One large and spreading fruit tree took up a third of the lawn. I enjoyed climbing into its main fork of branches and sitting there, surveying the rest of the garden. Privacy and freedom were the main elements of this holiday: I was in my own world and could do what I liked without any official routine to control me, or my time.

The wide river took up most of my ventures out. From the small side streets it was a few minutes walk to reach the water, just down below the old St Wilfrid's Church and its ancient graveyard. I wanted to swim in the inviting water but knew from Mum's and Frank's stories that it could be dangerous in the middle. Cows would be swept down it during flood times. The flat fields were only a few feet above the summer low of the water; I could imagine the river sweeping down in full flow, from the heavy rains of winter time, and spreading into flood over the pasture land.

This would be my last visit to the Ribchester home. I never knew at the time that Mum and Gran would be planning to move out, but they did. I returned from this time of sunshine and casual next-door friendships, to Barrows Green. I was missing Michael and my other friends there, anyway.

12

THE RADIO AND CINEMA

Dick Barton, Special Agent.

It was in the hut, by the orchard, where we stayed for two nights, when the dormitories were being painted. Sleeping on the shiny composite floor, only with blankets, we were allowed to have a radio on; this was a huge novelty. Radio Luxemburg's pop songs lulled us to sleep, and the warmth of the hut room gave comfort, regardless of the hard floor. Another world was somewhere out there, through the songs and the ease of the chatty broadcaster. And added to this new aural world, were the exciting caper, and the music, of Dick Barton Special Agent and his mate, Snowy. As my current catchphrase, I would imitate the introduction music and spoken line, "Dick Barton Special Agent", and go on with a spatter of action-words in the speed and tone of the narrator's radio voice. These late evenings and nights were a time of happiness for me – a time of imagination and freedom. I found some discarded ladies clothes and dressed up a bit, putting on a shawl. Most of all I enjoyed strutting about in Matron's black high heels shoes – though they were far too big, but they cluck-clicked on the floor. I imagined myself as powerful and important as Matron. But these hut-stay days were soon over; and the cosiness of the night-time gathering became swallowed up by the return to the worn routine of living in the main house.

One autumn day Master took a small group of us, travelling in the Home's green Austin of England van, across hilly countryside, through stormy weather, to see *Great Expectations*. It was shown in another Home, a large and daunting place, bigger than Barrows Green. By the time we arrived there it was dusk. In black and white, the film was scary and intense. The whole trip out impressed on my mind. Then we travelled back, and I was glad to be in the familiar safety of our Home.

In winter we were indoors, playing in the large playroom and having, sometimes, Master retelling stories from adventure books for us. One evening a week we had films in the large dining room: Sabu in the jungle, or black and white cowboy films, *Gunga Din*, or even *Batman*, or *Ali Baba and the Forty Thieves*. These latter two films I liked because of their secret caves: the image of the hidden door that opened in the rock at Ali Baba's command, with him on his horse, riding inside; and Batman's underground rooms – both heroes with unknown, private worlds that I hankered to be within. Some Saturdays we went to the local cinema; it was there, or in the Home, that we saw the serial films of Tom Mix, Gene Autry and Hopalong Cassidy; these characters were also in the comics that were scattered about the playroom. Gabby Hayes I found funny as an eccentric guy in the black-line drawn pictures. The *Eagle* comic, glossy and full of colour, I used to ask to see as only the Master's son got that; I found the green-coloured Mekon man, floating around on a type of personal hovercraft, interesting. The earth captain and other characters of this comic seemed, and looked like, blocks of wood, inexpressive and staid with their bubbles of speech. Dan Dare and Dennis the Menace I found curious and fun but one of, I think, the Scottish comic characters, some sort of human duck-looking creature, a bit frightening. There were many small, worn out, square comic books about, with war picture stories in them, all in plain line drawings – no colour.

In other story-pictures I could not work out why the German soldiers always behaved in a stupid way. They were drawn with senseless features – looking like fools – with block-shaped heads, wearing square helmets. How they were drawn and their behaviour did not feel right to me, but I did not try to work out why.

Zane Grey stories had imposing cowboy characters, but apart from looking at the front cover picture of the books, I did not know what the contents were about, not being that interested in reading them.

I cannot recall even seeing a dictionary or knowing what one meant. Yet one House Master, Mr Lewis, showed me his writings – many pages of blue ink. Within me stirred an affinity with him; he must have known of my love for writing and seen me often, alone in the large playroom at a small table, copying out rows and rows of numbers for Master, helping with his office work.

Mr Lewis also showed me photographs of wide streets in Calcutta, India. There lay about, on the sides, blankets containing sleeping people, very poor; they looked like bodies left, not thought of, or cared for, by anyone. These pictures impressed on my mind; I wanted to enter them – be there, with those stilled shapes of life.

For most of the summer evenings at the Home we climbed trees after tea time, or scampered in the fields. Rarely, I would go with the Master's son to see a film in one of the town's cinemas: not the small one, tucked away in a narrow winding street, which had a mysterious air about it, but the larger cinema, in one of the main streets. There I saw *How to Marry a Millionaire*. I could not work it out. It puzzled me, the joy and sunshine coming from Marilyn Monroe. I did not feel such apparent happiness, even though I was a little older than my *Great Expectations* days. Similarly, at an outing with a group of local supporters of the Homes, in the sunshine at Morecombe Bay, though I had an ice cream, and the company of joyful, and brightly dressed, women, I was not joyful. Looking up to their smiling faces and their open mouths of laughter, I could not work out the happiness of their behaviour, or the excited chatter of their voices. Deep inside me, I was weighted with sombre sorrow, not understood: that was my essential existence.

13

KENDAL: WEEKEND VISITS AND NEW SCHOOL

At school: headmaster states, Eric has worked quite well and made useful progress. He must work hard to improve his reading and spelling. This boy is emotionally handicapped.

In the buzz and jumble activity of these days I had to sit for the 11+ examination. Who would go to Kendal town's grammar school and who would go to the secondary modern school, also in the nearby town? Mr Johnstone, our headmaster, told me, much to my disappointment and unhappiness, that I had just failed the test, because of my spelling: I would be off to the secondary modern school. I felt second class, of no value. I believed myself to be as of the same quality as Andrew, the Master's son – he was going to the grammar school (but he also had lots of books to read at the Home *and* his own radio to listen to at any time he liked).

'What will you do when you're older?' Andrew asked me. The suddenness of this question, one morning, on a Saturday, when I was daydreaming on the cosiness of his bed, stunned my mind. I was eleven years old, nearly twelve, and starting at my secondary modern school.

'I don't know. What do you mean?'

'I'm going to be a teacher. We will do Latin at the grammar school.'

"Latin" was as mysterious to me as the letters of the sign in front of the ancient school. (Not that I realised that the family names of the little *Observer Book of Birds* I often carried around with me at Barrows Green were in Latin.) But that life inside a grammar school was not mine – I envied it, but at the time, I could not put such a word to the pain in my breast.

What would I do? My mind couldn't grasp such a vision, of a "future"; I barely was aware of my present circumstances. The fuzz and mist of my mental world had no room for a logical, planned framework of time; I could not work out the confusion within me. The field, the birds, insects and flowers were the only reference points of my world, above the disturbing yet pleasing awareness of my body and other boys' bodies. My existence became a strain between what I ought to be, in ideal and behaviour, and what I could see and feel in my daily life. There was not much to make sense of all this. My mind could not think to see clearly. To get through each day was sufficient – and I feared for my future.

'Don't you want to be a teacher – or something like that?'

'I suppose,' I answered with an image of several of my secondary modern school instructors in mind

– none of whom I desired to imitate. But they were the only adult people I had to copy, outside the Home, when I too would be grown up.

On these school days, I gazed longingly at this grammar building's gated entrance, and the boys with their smart green blazer and badge, as the bus I sat on passed further on into town. The mystery and potential of that school was not for me. I was off to an inferior quality school instead.

At least, most of the other Home's boys went to the same school as I, including Robert. And at lunchtime breaks he would take me across the road to reveal to me the workings of the world. After crossing over the River Kent, he introduced me to the foundry where his older brother worked, though the brother did not take an interest in my curiosity of the workings of things. Robert knew a bit about the business there, and showed me the big black sand-like moulds accepting the silvery liquid metal, forming massive angular shapes. That metal could melt and run like this intrigued me, as did the whole manly set-up, and atmosphere, of the foundry workplace.

During another school lunchtime hour, Robert took me to the projector room of one of the local cinemas. He and the projectionist showed me how the machinery worked: the bright rod that lit the film, the large reels of film, in flat, round tin containers. He got me to touch the totally frozen ice box and have my fingers stuck (in panic), the box seemingly burning me – another discovery of life: that ice had such power, and stung the flesh like heat. Also a visit to the slaughterhouse: the sight of a cow being stunned (on its forehead) also stunned my sensibility and I soon backed away out of this place. Robert showed me the salmon levels at the local weir; we watched them leaping upstream, high in the air; and we hung around the open trucks watching the crates of ice-dripping fish laid up in the riverside lorry park. The lorries there had come from far away, from some distant coast, and stayed over an hour or so in the town, on their way to their places of delivery.

And, from that position by the river, I watched as Robert waved to the row of girls from their school on the other side: the implied meaning of male and female need: he, as other boys, calling over the separating border of the river to the girls standing opposite at the railings there, and waving back. Like the boys' secondary modern, theirs was a single-sex school; it was strange, life was always males in the Homes and the school; girls were creatures apart, though we also had females as our House Parents, and our Matron. Females were an undiscovered mystery to me, about which I was mildly curious. As a peer group they did not enter into my life, least not till I began going to an adoptive aunt and uncle, Marian and Henry, each Saturday in the town.

From their local church, the Methodist church in Kendal, Henry and Marian had visited the Home, as they wished to give a selected child a taste of family home-life. Several of us were in line as the two visitors looked upon us. We had no idea why we were so lined up and under observation.

'The little lad there.' Marian pointed to me.

'Go on, Eric,' Master said, with a smile to Henry and Marian.

I hesitantly edged toward them, and stopped.

'Off you go, Eric.' Master tapped me on my bottom and gently pressed me to move. (Of the future, such a bottom tap I would have desired, to encourage me to take necessary steps, but there would be no accompaniment of Master to mentor me; I would be on my own.)

Here and now: reluctantly I went – and so began my weekend visits, thereafter travelling on my own, to Marian and Henry's home, not far from the Methodist church which I knew anyway, at the bottom of Windermere Hill, just through the town.

Halfway up the long hill there was a small road, like a lane, and through this I saw the slope of green of Kendal Green. It looked inviting; I desired to explore it, but I did not have courage enough to veer off my mission – to get to the Hallgarth Circle house of Marian and Henry's so the Green's mystery held its secret from me – and I walked up, onward.

The house had a steep back garden with a centre lawn rising up higher; I had dreams of water flooding down this slope to the gulley space at the base of the house. And there the dream ended; I did not know where the water eventually went – but it worried me in my dream.

The family had two daughters: Clare was much younger than me and the older one, Sandra, a year my junior. I used to pull her pigtails but did not otherwise play with her, preferring playmates I was familiar with, boys, the local ones, whom she knew, living nearby, especially a lively boy named Roger. As well as his adventurous ways, I was attracted to his handsome, dark-haired appearance.

One Saturday we all met with Clare's granddad, for an afternoon out, near Ambleside. He stood silent, neat in his check suit, beige and light green, with a small flower buttonhole. I looked up at his secure stance; I wanted his appearance of security – the strength I felt he had; a certainty of his place in the order of life. If he could be my father, and I could hug him tight to me, I would be strong also.

Through this adoptive aunt's family I did have a taste of family life. I went with them, in their car on Saturday, if Henry was not at his work, to little outings to town; or only with uncle, as I used to call him, to watch hill-track racing, putting myself in a dreamy state while sitting on the hillside listening to the regular low, then high, drone of the motors climbing up and round the hairpin bends.

With them and their church group, we had a summer trip out to an old stone barn, far into the countryside. The stand-alone barn was large and half full of yellow hay. We romped and played in the loose hay by the stored bales, and ran in the sunshine around the picnic side of the building. My heart filled with happiness at such sunshine and family-like freedom: other families with their children joining in; the cheery chatter and laughter, and the picnic food; and the adults, friendly and organising everything. All was secure and ordered. It was a day to remember.

We, in winter time, sang "The Happy Wanderer" around aunt's piano in their parlour, a very smart room kept only for Sundays and visitors, the settees and upholstery looking brand new and feeling stiff, the room smelling cool and unlived in. One weekend, I was shown, in the outhouse, a basket full of kittens. Yet I see myself at these visits still an outsider, looking on at the family's activities, even as I attempted to partake and emotionally enjoy their presence and family life. Important for me was to be in the kitchen, and stand nearby while auntie cooked; for some reason I preferred this time to anything else on my Saturday visits – with her reassuring smiles.

Some afternoons I spent time riding down the curving steep road where the family lived, at the bottom. I would gather speed and dare myself to keep on the large scooter, with both feet on the stand, and barely holding onto the tiny handlebar; but three-quarters of the way down I would step on the back wheel brake bar, just as the scooter started to wobble and become uncontrollable, the danger exhilarating me. After finishing the run, I'd walk the way back to the house, enlivened and happy about my personal achievement. The older one of the daughters had tried this long hill, but she had fallen off and cut herself.

Months later, Clare and I took a shortcut through the cattle market, which was open that day. We, or rather Clare, got wolf whistles and smiles from the men standing about, and some leaning on the animal pens. I felt their attention, initially, was for me, and so got hot and bothered. I soon realised the light-hearted attention was for Clare. Even so, I walked stiffly beside her and was glad when we came onto the street, from where we met up with Marian. And we all finished our trip into town by getting the car back to their house. From this experience I knew that Clare was not only my weekend play friend but someone whom men were attentive to because she was female. Yet this was a thing I vaguely understood: men attended to women in some different, important way; and that this way did not feel to be in me.

*

There were days when I did not get to my secondary modern school till hours later, especially if I had missed the bus; and in winter I would have to trudge through high piles of drift snow till eventually, two miles away, the clearer town roads would mark my way. My lateness to school, and my delay in seeking the correct class, did not seem to get me into any trouble.

I was in the "A" stream, yet I was detached from the flow of chat and emotional interaction at this older boys' school, and was quiet much of the day.

The Home's Master, Mr Savidge, once showed me one of my school reports: "This boy is emotionally handicapped". I did not understand this description, thinking only of "handicapped" meaning not being able to walk. Nothing, to my awareness, was acted upon this knowledge, by the Home – and I continued on my emotionally insular existence, most notably at school. At games time I stood on the boundary and watched the others at play: they were objects, moving or standing – and I was left to my own condition, an invisible wall within me, separating any possible feeling between them and myself. The practical lessons were also strange for me: I stood and watched in the sheet metal work class, the tools and metal appearing very hard and dangerous. I managed a bit of woodwork, the wood having a sense of friendliness.

English lessons I enjoyed and was more confident in, though I was graded as "average" there, which used to surprise me as in my hazy reckoning I thought that I was better than other classmates higher up the grades. But the headmaster stated on my school report:

> Eric has worked quite well and made useful progress. He must work hard to improve his reading and spelling.

Music was a fascinating mystery to me: that one of the other boys knew what the squiggles meant, a "crotchet", baffled me. History and Geography, as well as English, interested me, and Technical Drawing. I could not work out why we could not spend all our time on these subjects: one day for each – and I saw as confusing the moving from one class, one lesson, to another every hour or so; it was, anyway, like a child migration throughout the school, up and down dark cold stone stairs, crowding and jostling in the dim passageways.

Maths was interesting but the teacher, Mr Jones, seemed always to be angry, and so was scary. The sky and moving clouds, outside the tall windows, took a lot of my attention during his class, much to his fury.

I did focus on the blackboard for the intriguing Pi r-squared formula which was also twenty-two over seven, as a fraction. The combination of numbers contrasted to the circle shape interested me, just because it puzzled me.

Often I was uncomfortable in class: my dick frequently stiff, and if I wanted the toilet, too scared to put up my hand to be excused, and if I occasionally did so, I received the cross response: 'Can't you wait for break time, boy?'

One day the urgency was too much and I boldly put up my arm to ask to go. Knowing there would be resistance, by the teacher, I added urgency to my request: 'Please sir, I really need to go!' And even as I spoke I was about to pee in my pants.

'Go on then boy, and be quick about it!'

So I scrambled between desks, very aware of the

tightness of my dick in my pants, and blushing, self-conscious of other boys, looking at me.

I entered the fresh air and walked for several minutes to the outside toilets. They were empty and I was free in my private world. Even so, my dick was too stiff to be able to pee, and I waited ages till any came out.

While standing there, in the white-tiled silence, I saw a grubby milk bottle hanging up with string, from the water pipe. After I had finished peeing I lifted the bottle and peered inside. All I could see was some pale liquid. A note was scrawled on a piece of paper stuck to the outside – but I could not understand its meaning – and left the bottle hanging there.

Later on in the day, a short talk by one of the teachers was addressed to the class. I felt it was directed at me and my visit to the toilet that day, but did not understand the import of his message. However, I sensed it had some importance as the milk bottle and its contents was "a serious offence and must not be allowed to happen again".

Years later, I could understand the contents of the bottle, as no doubt the senior boys of the school could do so, for they could produce sperm, as I could not.

I was, though, becoming aware of a larger world, outside the Home. I mixed with older boys, fleetingly, and began to understand "rules" and physical "punishment"; that one shouldn't shout out teachers' nicknames – not even from the cover of a bus. "Phew!" was not acceptable for Mr Hugh. A slap on the face by the headmaster, in his study, each culprit boy, including me, one by one in line – his hand like the passage of a missile over our frightened faces – was the punishing result of juvenile play or, in secondary modern school rules: "overstepping the boundary of civility". Yet another time I was mysteriously called in to Mr Hugh's classroom, one lunch period: 'Put your hand out,' he instructed.

'Why?' I asked, shocked and confused.

'You know why. Come on, put your hand out.' He had beside him, pressed to his trouser leg, a small cane.

I refused, knowing I had not done anything wrong. We stood a while staring at each other, he with an angry, exasperated expression.

'Get out!' he shouted.

I sulkily left his empty classroom, knowing he had made a mistake. Someone, I began to reason, had been calling out his nickname, but it was not me.

I was impish at times, and had to eat sandwiches, made at the Homes, for flicking some paper across my dining room table at lunchtime. This hit me hard, emotionally, to sit all alone in the gallery high above the assembly floor of dining tables, while everyone else had the regular school meal below. This punishment seemed a totally unfair treatment of my misdemeanour – I felt the teachers were cruel and barbaric in their lack of sensitivity; most were like alien people to me. Apart from the English teacher who appeared friendly, though we nicknamed him "sticky lips" due to his thick, and seemingly always sore, lips. The history master appeared benign, large and stolid; and the natural history or "science" master, fun, because of his large, scruffy appearance, and slightly eccentric behaviour – often seemingly sharing a private joke with himself – and even more interesting was that he looked after the school's beehives.

14

LOSS OF FACE

Home and Colonial.

'Your mother is coming Friday. I've given a note for school. You will have to be here beforehand, in case she arrives a day earlier; she was not certain what day,' Matron told me in a cross-sounding voice, one Tuesday.

I was glad, fearful and excited. I couldn't recall the last time I had received a visit from her – six months, even a year – but such calendar spans were timeless, and almost forgettable as a child.

Staying in at the Home for the day, and separated out from my friends, I was a bit self-conscious – like I had some disease. I felt I was betraying the other boys – even the Home – for "parents" to visit was as if strangers were descending, interfering in the life of the orphanage. But the day arrived: it was Easter Good Friday – and the other boys were at the Home anyway, in the playroom. I had to wait in the hallway, by myself, for my mother to arrive. Matron appeared around the passage corner. 'Your mother's coming at an awkward time.' She spoke this to me in passing. Hours had gone by since breakfast time, and since then the other boys had left the playroom, rushing by me in excitement: they were going on a walk. Returning from her sitting room Matron addressed me again: 'You had better get your mac – she may take you out. Tell your mother to bring you back by four, if you still want to go to the service.'

'Yes, I will.' I got a sharp pang of pain in my stomach on the contradiction this situation presented to me: the demands, indeed attractions, of the day out with my mother (however a "distant" person as she was to me) and the more powerful commitment to keep my attendance at Master's Good Friday evening service. I decided I *would* get back in good time for Master.

'Hello, Eric. How are you, luv?' Her Lancashire accent was friendly. She stood – loomed – large over me. I stood up, my height barely reaching her chest.

'All right, thank you.' Politeness seemed the correct procedure of reply, especially as my mother was a formal person in appearance to me – and I didn't feel any exchange – or very little – of warmth from her.

'I'll let Matron know I'll be taking you out for the day…'

'I want to be back for church with Master.'

'I will ask Matron.'

'Matron knows,' I called to my mother as she walked, without a concern about my information, to Master's sitting room.

We left soon after – I was fully dressed for the early springtime weather, and Mother was in her everlasting dark blue overcoat (I forever visualise her wearing this outer garment). We travelled by taxi to the railway station, then an hour's travel or so, to Lancaster.

Apart from the Home & Colonial Store, when we sat on the high stools awaiting service, and the splendid array of cakes filled my eyes, and the surrounding liveliness of the place, with objects, colour and brightness everywhere, in a world which overpowered my senses, full of sound and the bustle of people; what stood out in my memory of the day were the grey blocks of stone buildings of the main streets, and the bleak emptiness, without the company of my Home friends. I was being guided here, by my mother, yet I did not have much to say to her. She had little to converse with me: 'Would you like something to eat?' or 'We need to return soon.' We had some difficulty travelling back, as mother had a problem with money. I didn't really understand this – as money was to me "pocket money", money was for saving. I didn't fully realise that it was the vital means to do everything; that it was like a smiling face – it would get you everywhere in the shops and on transport – that without it you were faceless – unrecognised.

In trying to give me a happy time, my mother had spent too much money, and did not have enough to pay the fares to get us back.

My mother was short of it – and she looked helpless and weak – and as confused as I was. A police car finally solved the question of my return to the Home.

I heard my mother, in sorrowful voice, telling the desk sergeant of her plight. I was meek on seeing the cold-shouldering of my mother's importance that day; her loss of face was mine too.

We missed the time of my expected return. I therefore did not attend the Good Friday service. That's how I remember my mother's Good Friday visit – and the lesson in the meaning of "money".

The unhappiness of this day was compounded by Matron's evening remark – just before my bedtime: 'I don't see how your mother can buy a house to take you there to live when she can't even pay for the train!'

If my mother was planning such a thing I would fear it, for the only safety I had was at Barrows Green. The outer world was still too far beyond me; without the other boys I would be all by myself in the world. Yet at my age, approaching thirteen, my horizons *were* opening up; and even the unhappiness of the secondary modern school would soon be a thing of the past.

15

NEW HORIZONS: WILLIAM BAKER TECHNICAL SCHOOL

*Interested to hear Eric would like to go to Goldings,
there is some gardening there but more boys than
vacancies. Is there anything else boy would like to do?
Send full report on lad and opinion from headmaster
as to what boy is fitted for.*

A month before Christmas the Home had a visit: a smartly dressed older boy, aged seventeen, entered our smaller world. He showed us a sun-filled movie film of the life of the Home *he* belonged to: William Baker Technical School; this school was also known as "Goldings". There we could gain a training in a trade (learn how to do things, make or grow things – and so to earn our future living). It all looked enticing, especially for me: the splendid blossom-filled gardens, with cherry-faced gardeners busy at work, some with cheeks as large and rounded as autumn apples about to fall at harvest time; and espalier fruit (as I was taught later) decorating the sun-splashed orange-brick walls, all appeared to be paradise in this walled garden. I was enraptured.

NEW HORIZONS: WILLIAM BAKER...

The smart-suited senior boy from William Baker Technical School was here at Barrows Green, recruiting for boys to join his Home and learn a trade. I was keen on doing gardening: "horticulture" as the Goldings boy said. My interest in plants, as well as insects, was great, ever since the time I had been given my own little patch of garden.

Letter to Mr Savidge from Area Office:

> Interested to hear Eric would like to go to Goldings, there is some gardening there but more boys than vacancies.
>
> Is there anything else boy would like to do? Send full report on lad and opinion from headmaster [secondary modern school] as to what boy is fitted for.

Mr Savidge replied:

> Eric is very interested in nature and gardening; gardening is what he must do.

My decision to go to this training Home was made definite in my mind when my brotherly friend, Robert, applied to seek his future there. He left within weeks. I was at a loss, but had to wait till the coming of springtime when I would be over thirteen years of age and then old enough to start there. Other friends of my age group were applying also.

9.3.1954   Letter to Mr Savidge, Kendal, stating
Eric accepted for Goldings and will
be transferred at Xmas term (Robert
Peach also accepted).

The months did go by, and I departed to a new kind of life, without a thought to my past, or my present point of departure, for Barrows Green was slipping away – my eye, my imagination, was looking to a future dreamland.

'But what about Michael?' Sandra, the older daughter of the Saturday "aunt" of my adopted family asked me, only weeks before I would leave for Hertfordshire.

I hadn't given him a thought – such was the attraction of a future, to reach somewhere else. 'He's your best friend, isn't he?' I said nothing – only visualised him, his curly ginger hair and his buck-tooth smile – then his freckled face faded from my mind.

Being driven down the lane, I looked over at the passing fields; a tractor alone was working on the horizon. My journey toward my new Home had begun.

* * *

William Baker Technical School stood splendid in its pale orange-brick stature as a mock Jacobean country house. It was donated to Dr Barnardo's Homes before my arrival on the scenes of its lawns and playing fields.

As well as the main house on higher land, the nearby sloping grounds were occupied with the buildings of the workshops, which housed the previous owner's stables. In this cluster of buildings boys learnt their trade: carpentry, printing, and cobbling repairs or, in another site of buildings and land area, my choice: horticulture.

'Collect your boots and get your school blazer and grey trousers from the stores, by the ablution block,' Mr Warren, one of the junior boys' House Parents, told me. I duly followed his instructions and walked across the parade ground to get there, arriving in minutes, excited and a little nervous, not knowing exactly what to expect from all this adult-like formality of procedure.

'Here, this should be about your size,' the stores man said. And so he repeated this phrase on all the clothes I was directed to try on, and eventually walk away with, after he took my name and House, even though I could see that he had the required information on his list. Now I was acquiring a new identity: at Barrows Green my number was twenty-two, here it was one hundred and thirty-three.

22.9.1954   Letter to mother, stating boy now at
              William Baker Technical School
              (Goldings).

Over two hundred boys was a large company to get used to, after living with less than thirty, as was the hundred

139

or so stone steps spiralling up one of the two towers –
this tower, to reach the top floor juniors' dormitories –
my first house of rest, named Buxton House.

I wrote to my mother in excitement telling her of
the many stone steps to get to my dormitory; of the
number of boys here. She replied, concerned for my
health at having to climb such a large stairway. But
this was a different life for me, expanding my
imagination as well as the activity of my body; all
was a new and broadening landscape of Home's life.

The lawns and cricket pitches were kept
manicured and in good order. So too, we were kept
in order, by daily bugle calls (the overall discipline
of the Home being run on army barrack lines: parade
ground grouping before meals, Reveille call to get up
in the morning, and Last Post at sundown). I did not
like the line-up and parades into Houses before
meals and the marching in. We were treated as
groups not as individuals, unlike Barrows Green.
Even in our dormitories, we were held responsible:
to strip our beds down in the morning and to build
a neat bundle of sheets and blankets, at the foot end,
for inspection by the House Master. Nor did I like the
activity of polishing the dormitory wood floor each
morning: the pink slimy "Ronuk" polish was also
used as an initiation ceremony for junior boys
moving down to the older boys' rooms: it was
plastered around the individual's private parts. It did
not happen to me; certainly I was frightened at the
thought of facing this public rite.

There was no privacy; even though we had our own lockers, all stuff of personal value (or rather, of value to other boys) would be stolen. After getting up from bed we would make our way down the never-ending, tower-winding, stone steps, popping out into the hall then across to the side door and out to the parade ground; running over this to the ablution block, we were ready for our ablutions. Here we stripped to our waists and washed ourselves in basins, all lined up, with a parallel set of basins opposite, and so, head to head, we busied ourselves with splashing and towelling. High on one wall a large shiny metal mirror was fixed, giving a blurry image of our faces when combing our hair. Then breakfast in the low-roofed newer side-building. Afterwards back to the dormitories, and standing by our beds for inspection, mainly for the tidiness of our bundled-up blankets. From this duty we made our way to the morning assembly; there prayers, a hymn and a comment of what had happened recently, or was planned to happen for the day, by the headmaster, before he departed. Then we left the assembly room, in an organised fashion, to our schooling, or workshops, or rarely, some duty or other to perform for that day.

Robert was just still in the juniors' dormitories but in another House to me, Pelham. I had not been at Goldings long and Robert took me exploring one late evening onto the small roof just outside the Master's workroom. We were hidden in the dark, and being of the level of Mr Warren's window made our escapade the more exciting: we could hear the occupants' talk but we were hidden away from the yellow light-spread of the room. Our movement over the roof, though, attracted the attention of Mr Warren: he called out, 'Who's there on the roof? Come on in.'

I was frightened of punishment, to be caught out of bounds, roof-climbing; I was about to get up but Robert whispered to me: 'Get down, stay quiet.' I lay low, not looking as he got up and made his way to the window: 'It's me, sir.'

'Get inside now,' I heard Mr Warren's deep voice demand.

I kept very still, scared I too would be claimed by Mr Warren. Robert had sacrificed himself for my safety; I was thankful but could not really understand why he had done this for me. It was over half an hour, or longer, before I dared make my way back into the main building and safety. I never even found out what punishment Robert had been given – and he never told me, the night's sleep and the routine of activity of the next day bringing forgetfulness of the matter – and not seeing Robert, as his dormitory was away from mine, and his trade being sheet-metal work, our pathways would not cross often, and not during the daytime.

At the top of the castle-like building our floor was cosy and comfortable in the dark winter days. Mr Warren's office was always open for boys to go in and out, there being a small gathering clustered, busy in some questioning and chattering, or doing odd jobs. The yellow lights filled the dormitories of an evening; and from Mr Warren's radio, the ballads of David Whitfield singing, vibrated the air. On hearing his voice, I would sing out spontaneously. I particularly liked "Cara Mia", and always rose to the occasion to join the melody. The bubbly voice of Alma Cogan I liked also – and her popular song, "Dreamboat", I would sing out to, too. Even with these short interludes of singing, I could not always settle down, as the other boys seemed to. I would wander about the dormitories and passageways, conscious that I *was* wandering; that I appeared as a stray animal, just outside the company of the many domesticated ones. Then I was at a loss – being lost in myself. At such times, the sharing of this environment and society was strange to me.

Mr Lewis sent me a greetings card, saying he hoped that I was happy at Goldings. On reading the card, and seeing his familiar, large handwriting, a pang of loss hurt me – and that he did not have an address on the card added to my small sorrow (I thought, for some reason, that he was no longer at Barrows Green). I could not reply to him; he did not ask me to – so I lost him, and had to get on with my new life (which soon took over my memories of Barrows Green, anyway).

Compared to Barrows Green, the routine of daily life was entirely different at Goldings. Gone was the family atmosphere of the previous, smaller Home.

Here the boys were of ages from thirteen and a half to sixteen, and the print shop apprentices, who were occasionally seen, of seventeen.

One of the older boys, in a small gathering of us, standing around joking and chatting, tickled his finger in the centre of my palm. I giggled; the boy's smiles and proximity excited me. Robert was nearby as I happened to squirm close to him. 'Keep away from him,' Robert whispered, 'he's a shirt-lifter.' I fell sullen – my fun was spoilt by the sobriety of this information; some boundary he had advised against crossing, but I could not formulate what it was exactly. I did not want to show the sudden dilemma within me to my brotherly friend. I wanted the tickling and the attraction of this curly-haired boy, and the fun he gave me, to continue, but I could not go against Robert's direction and the danger I sensed in his warning. But this personal disturbance soon dissipated into the variety of the new environment and school activity about me.

Daily habits were governed by army ritual, and of all the bugle calls, I found a liking to the melancholy sound of the "Last Post". With the day's routine finished, the Union Jack would be lowered slowly, and everybody on or near the parade ground stood still till the tune was played out, and the flag fully descended. Then boys would scatter quickly to their individual ways, free from the enforced minutes of reflection.

We assembled in blocks, on the parade ground, before marching into the food hall for our meals. All this depersonalisation I resented, though it seemed to fade from its heavy first impact on my nature. As time went on, after a year or two, we did not have to assemble together before each meal to be counted, to see if we were all present; and for this I was glad.

In my first year at Goldings, and fresh from the freedom of Barrows Green life, I was perky and inquisitive, sometimes calling names to older boys, safe in the knowledge that I was able, by my nippy youth, to run away, and this fleeing, accompanied by my high laughter jerking out, at the excitement of potentially being caught. Though one particular tease was to a senior boy with a gammy leg; if I was caught by him I would be truly thumped; there was more danger with him but also more chance of escape from him.

'Are you Jewish?' a senior boy came up to me, with other boys about on the parade ground, during early evening free time. I looked at him, puzzled. 'Your big nose,' he said.

I did not know what to say, but the little jingle I knew from Barrows Green days: "All Jews have long noses, including Moses," played through my mind. 'No,' I responded, my voice sounding a querulous pitch. We stared at each other. He walked away; the group of boys nearby dispersed, leaving me alone for a moment. *I must be special*, intimated a thought, then I slipped off into the general melee of my age group, all running about.

Such things were minor to the expanse offered to my imagination from my new life and its environment. It all helped in the opening up of my mind: the greater space of the Home, the vast increase of boys, and the regimentation of the routine, and, of course, the world of trade learning.

The manners of the dining hall were rough: the older boys taking the food off younger ones, as they felt like. This unfairness stirred my feelings, but I was helpless to protest, for all was confusing to me, and I was a new boy, and such behaviour appeared accepted routine. At times there were "food fights" with bread and goodness knows what thrown everywhere. The only one I partly experienced was in my earlier days at the Home. I had gone out of the dining room on some small errand, or was just very late getting in for my meal, I can't remember, but I recall how, when approaching the heavy old door, from inside the main building corridor, a roar of shouting and noise came out.

'Don't go in there at this moment,' one of the senior House Parents told me, on suddenly coming up behind (I guessed he must have been called to help in the control of the riot of behaviour). I waited back in the corridor, and went in much later, to see the disarray of benches, and boys at work with buckets and mops cleaning, and other boys sullenly sitting at the bench tables on the backless forms. I don't recall having any food myself at that particular meal time. I was swept in with the punishment of the whole room, and the rest of the meal period was cancelled.

Just about this time, I was selected to collect from the main kitchen and serve the headmaster's lunch in his study. The meal would be neatly laid out on the tray and covered with metal lids for me to carry along the cold, stone-flagged corridor. Thankfully, at this same time the school were in the dining hall having their lunch. To meet up with the other boys in the crowd and rush would be tricky. Apart from any deliberate jostling that would happen, I found, as it was, the effort to carefully walk and carry the food tray an awkward and precarious duty.

Through this diligence and care of collection and serving the headmaster's weekday lunch, I was given the occasional duty of doing odd jobs in his apartment, at the top of the wide formal stairs (the stairs to all the boys' dormitories was up a spiral of stone steps, within a tower – the general staff having another stairway, not grand at all but functional, near the rear of the home). Across the polished wide hallway – which completely separated the headmaster's apartment from access by way of heavy swing doors, from the boys' dormitories – then through small doors and into the expanse of sitting room, the double bedroom and bathroom, I would take the headmaster's polished ankle boots for cleaning, or dust around here and there, his bedroom and lounge. Once I passed near his son's bedroom, its door partly opened. Music was playing, the song from

the musical *Carousel* filled the air, a sweet female voice
sang: "And when the children are asleep, we'll
dream". I peeped inside the room – its colour of
pictures and posters on the walls hit me hard; the
room was full of interest and excitement, books and
patterns of clothes everywhere – and the record
player, with the song sound turning round and round.
My heart was weighted with a sense of loss – I was
envious too, my emotions all mixed up. I became
confused, being happy to see this Aladdin's Cave, but
also deeply disappointed. I had none of this, I was in
a prison, in the dormitories, where all this entitlement
was denied me; my hurt told me it was supposed to
be for me too. I was equal, I judged, to the
headmaster's son. And the words of the song brought
back to me the room of personal comfort and
individuality that Andrew possessed at Barrows
Green – each son was privileged to a life I could not
have, and they took their life, their own private world,
with such ease, as if it were their natural right, and I
could not understand this. Their lifestyle was
abnormal to me, for mine was the familiar one, and so
too for all my peers. I stood and gazed at the contents
of the room for as long as I dared – before my stillness
and silence from activity would call the attention of
the adults in the other rooms; I had to return to my
real existence, and so, moved back into my duties.

A time came when a Patron of the Homes, HRH
Princess Margaret, came to perform an official duty. I
served the headmaster and herself at teatime in his

study. Coming into the study and approaching the table, set with the backdrop of the landscape view across the huge lawn, the lower cricket field and the distant lake, I was shocked to see a long cigarette holder being held to the Princess's lips. Smoking was not allowed for the boys and to see such a provocative action being performed here by Princess Margaret, and in the headmaster's study (*why didn't he stop her?* I wondered)... after a moment of standing still, I moved forward and added sandwiches to the table and waited, looking at the table scene. 'That will be all, thank you, Eric,' the headmaster told me. This pleasant use of my first name surprised me too – though it pleased me, and I politely turned about and left the study.

Not many months later, this meal-time job of serving the headmaster ended. I was growing too big – also, inside my head and feelings, I struggled with my having to call the headmaster "sir". I too, I reasoned, was of equal worth as him, indeed, of all grown-ups, yet I had to respect his position. So I would struggle with this and, over time, gradually did not call anyone "sir" – but then, I was growing up too. Other work came up, outside the Home's gate.

Wanting a bit of extra pocket money, I joined a small gathering of youngsters to stand in a display line before the lady and her husband who lived in a bungalow tucked in the hill of Mole Wood, near to, but outside the grounds of Goldings. She stood, with cigarette in hand and dark red lipstick, beside her husband, he short and well fed, with a bushy moustache, a red-wine-filled glass in his hand and a fat cigar, both squashed together by his fleshy fingers, waited. 'Which one do you think, darling?' she asked her husband, while still glancing over our eager faces. She stopped at me. 'You look rather cute,' she said, after I had replied something cheeky to a question she had put to me. 'Yes, you can have the job,' she stated. I was pleased: there was nothing for the other boys and they had to make their way back to school. So, I immediately started the garden tidying-up job: gathering leaves and generally skivvying for her, fetching coffee and collecting up her and her husband's, empty wine glasses. They were the images of people my Methodist upbringing had warned me against, or rather against the wrongful doings, such as alcohol and smoking. Their indulgences and their indulgent way of life was something I had not encountered before, and they intrigued me as well as shocked. 'I have to go off to the London now sweetie,' the man told her later as he came out of the bungalow dressed up very smartly in black suit and black dickey tie; I imagined all the money they must have. I only worked there a couple of Saturday afternoons; the lady gave me a few shillings and that was that. 'We won't need you anymore,' she told me; 'the garden can look after itself, for the next few months.'

'All right, thank you,' I said and skipped my way, quite thankfully, out of their garden and into the wood's path, glad that I was free, as I feared her a little, thinking of her as some kind of witch.

The months following, I went through a period of adjustment, and my everyday liveliness and energy increased. Sometimes my body, at night-time, was so exhausted that I could not relax it to go to sleep, also with the mind still lively from the day's stimulation, the hourly buzz of so many other boys around me, and so much general noise and activity. But I survived and, as I approached my fourteenth year, I was coming into my own. I had moved down a floor, to the seniors, and entered Aberdeen House. By now I had stopped "wetting the bed". The oversized bedstead I previously slept on had stuck out like a sore thumb from the corner space of the juniors' annexe; and, being positioned near to the toilet, made me very aware of my failure to be like the other boys. Over the weeks I had consciously made the effort not to wet my bed. Like the ever-present sense of my being, I wanted to have control of my life, myself, to strive out of the fog of my earlier days of confusion. Also, the nightmares, of seeing bright, red-eyed devil-like creatures, staring at me from the dark corners of the bedroom ceiling, had stopped – and the night-time, intestinal jabs of pain, had ceased.

Now, in the seniors' world, I could not quite remember, or want to, of my little-boy past, but I knew still, that I wanted to reach out for something more, and let free something deep inside of me; it was like a very distant shore, of some island I desired to land on, through my imagination. Anyway, here I was livelier in myself, and had more space – to wander, to be lost to others, to be private and to still find interest, and solace, in the nature that surrounded the huge estate: rivers, woods, orchards and fields; the night walks by owl woods and whirring sounds of unknown wings – all for my intrigue and enjoyment. An occasional exploration of nature with one of my peer group soon petered out as he had little real interest in bird watching; it required too much waiting around for him, or "patience", as I understood it. One day our investigations led us into the apple storage sheds which in turn led to my being called to the headmaster's study, the following weekday morning. Someone in authority had seen us go into the shed. After an exploration of my whereabouts that morning, the headmaster vaguely asked me: 'The thing you were doing there?'

'We were just exploring,' I innocently replied.

'Jackson and yourself, in the shed?'

I thought of his study, and of his cane of punishment, and I stared at the fireguard stand with its tapestry display guard of a woven battle scene. The headmaster was trying to say something I could not grasp. I stood there seeking some answer in his face.

'Together...' the headmaster said, hinting at something.

'No!' I burst out, suddenly visualising me and Jackson embracing in the shed. It had dawned on me what he was trying to say.

He fixed me with his bespectacled eyes a long time: 'Well, be careful where you do your nature-watching.' He turned his attention to some table-top papers, rearranging and sliding them to the table edge near him. For a moment he appeared to have forgotten that I was in his study. Then he looked sideways, back to me: 'You can leave now,' he said.

And I left his study, disgruntled that he had almost accused me of doing something that was far from my actual occupation, nature-watching, on that day.

16

EARLY RESPONSIBILITY
AND HOME CHOICE

*Going home for Christmas request report: Mother whose
new home is not yet at all tidy and straight.*

'Hey, the headmaster wants you in his study,'
Allen, a House Senior, shouted out to me.

I was wandering off toward the chapel woods, not
that any of the boys were supposed to be around there,
outside Sunday church attendance. 'What! Me?' I was
scared that I had done something wrong, but could not
think what it was: out of bounds and playing about
with other boys whizzed through my imagination.

'Yes, you better get there quick. I've been ages
looking for you!'

So off I walked.

'You'd better run Holden if you don't want the
stick!' He laughed. I knew that I would not get the
cane, just for being late for something that I did not
know about. I skipped into a run then slowed down
around the corner but walked quickly to the side
door entrance, into the main hall.

I tapped carefully on the headmaster's study
door.

'Come in.' And I entered.

'Ah! Don't look so worried, I want you to do a little duty. Go to Hertford North Station and meet a new boy there; Mortimer is his name. You can both walk back.'

I gulped quietly and stiffened at such a burden: going out by myself to the station and then bringing back a boy, who would not be much younger than me, I thought.

'Yes, sir.' I was still reluctant to say "sir" as I considered that I was of the same importance as he; but I had to bottle up my frustration to express my feelings over this matter.

'Bring him to the office when you get back.'

I knew he had finished with his instructions and that he had done with me, when he turned to some papers on his large centre table. I imagined boys had to bend there, over its end edge, to get the cane.

'Yes, sir.' I turned and left the study.

I didn't think to tell anyone where I was going: I was on duty from the headmaster, so that was that, the occasion forced me to collect my senses and become very serious. The walk, a mile to the station, went quickly, and it was a sunny day, which eased my present duty. I did not take the usual shortcut that led into the back end of Hertford, passing the river – a walk I liked because of the forest of large trees banked up at one side, when past the ending of the river, at a pumping station. At times, if by myself, I would stop my walking and gaze up at the thick trunks and wonder what would be beyond them – not quite able to imagine where, or what, that would be. On this occasion, to get to the station, the shortcut would have been a long way round, for the station was not in the town itself but beside the main road, before the town. Arriving there, Mortimer was waiting in the entrance, at the bottom of the stairs. He looked like a Goldings boy already, somehow. He had a tiny suitcase with him.

'Come on, I have been told to take you to Goldings.'

'Yes,' was all he said.

We walked in silence – I could think of nothing to say all the way back along the main road and up the estate roadway and into the main building.

'I have to take you to the office.' I knocked on the office door and the Head of the Office, Mr Maslin, opened it, poking his grey head around.

'I've been told…' I started to say.

'Yes, I know, come on in Mortimer.' He entered and the door closed. I stood there a moment, wondering if I should report to the headmaster, but decided not, and walked off into the day. It was Saturday, so I, like the other boys, was in my own free time – though mine had been taken up with unexpected responsibility. I had a stiffening of pride though: I had been chosen to do that duty.

★ ★ ★

Expectation of my more grown-up status did not end there: Christmas came around, my mother had requested for me to go "home" for the holiday:

13.12.1954	Letter to Mr Wooldrage, Liverpool, asking him to visit mother and report re her wish to have boy home for Xmas holiday. Mother's address is 15 Beech Street, Fishergate Hill, Preston.
18.12.1954	Mrs Allen, Leyland, Lancashire, reports she visited mother, whose new home is not yet at all tidy and straight. There is a spare bedroom and beds available for Eric and brother Edward, who is expected home on 27th for a week. Mother is a kindly woman, and obviously fond of boys, so even though the house is not too good, Mrs Allen is sure she will do her best to give them a happy time, and it might be good for brothers to meet. Old Mrs Holden (Mrs Simpson) is very deaf and almost blind – she sleeps downstairs, and there are three bedrooms. Mother asks if boy will be able to travel alone. She will be ready for him by 22nd.

20.12.1954   Phoned Mr Wheatley and informed
             him that we agree to boy spending
             holiday with mother. He confirms can
             travel alone, and will inform mother
             by wire what time to expect boy in
             Preston.

This was strange as it was scary for me. "Home" had
become peculiarly distant in any meaning for me: my
emotional life was here, with the other boys and the
wide world of activities, the excitement and bustle.
Going to see my mother put me in an isolated position:
how should I behave? What was I supposed to do? Also,
I was now feeling a bit too old to go home to my mother.

'Your mother has a house now in Preston and she
would like you up there for a week. Do you want to
spend Christmas with your mother?'

The Office Head did not wait for an answer:
'Tomorrow morning come to the office and be
dressed in your Sunday clothes.'

My mind numbed without a thought working
through it. I stumbled up the stone steps to the
dormitory; I wondered then what "Preston" would
be like.

I was upright in my Sunday best as I tapped on
the office door: 'Here I am, Mr Maslin.'

'Ah, yes...'

I panicked a moment: had he forgotten me?

'Wait there.' And back he popped, behind the
closing door.

Again he appeared and handed me a small, stiff-card, rail ticket. It looked important, with cramped writing printed on both sides. 'This ticket will take you all the way and back again. Your mother will meet you at the station in Preston.' He passed to me a small sheet of paper. I glimpsed dates and clock times on it.

'Go now, and you will catch the next train from Hertford. All the train times and details are on that paper.'

He went back into the office. I stood a moment – I was alone, a weight of something pressed on my shoulders. I wanted to cry, yet I was nearing fourteen, not that I was really aware of what that meant, but I could not work out how and why I was expected to behave; no one had taught me. I'd better be off, I told myself, and this felt like another duty I had to perform: *go up to see your mother, catch the train…*

Somehow, by asking grown-ups, I got onto the right train and travelled up to Preston. All the way I sat in the same position, stiff and frightened. An old lady gave a little smile to me, which confused me, and I looked away after trying to work out what her politeness meant. I was glad to get off at Preston, and my muscles got working again.

I looked around, the station was large – metal girders, a dull reddish colour, rose high above me. I shivered in the cold air – I received no warmth or comfort from this impersonal place. Along the platform I stood upon I recognised my mother. I was glad to see her; at least I had completed my duty, and arrived.

'No one came up with me,' I told her.

'Well they said not for me to come down to collect you; that you were responsible enough to travel by yourself.'

I brightened up on seeing the evening lights and the Christmas decorations in the shops of Preston Town Centre; it all became exhilarating; a surge of freedom rushed through my body. I held my mother's hand for a moment, then became aware of what I was doing and let go; this was all so odd for me, and I did not know where or what my feelings were – or what they were meant to be.

The house had three small bedrooms, one my mum slept in and another, a front room, I slept in. Gran slept downstairs, her bed tucked into the corner on the fireside but opposite the backyard window. The smallness of the rooms, indeed the whole house, centred me into myself – my imagination had nowhere to go, after my life experience of home space in huge mansions and large grounds. This was home, and it was as strange as the feeling I tried to create, of closeness and family. Gran and Mum were my relatives, and again, what was I supposed to feel?

'Come and sit by the fire, Eric, you must be cold and tired after all that long journey.' Mum removed a towel, drying on the back of the seat she had offered me.

'Eee, I don't know how they send you all by

yourself,' Gran complained – 'all the way from London. Eee, I don't know.' I didn't know if she was speaking to me or my mum, but I kept looking at her as she pulled her shawl tighter over her shoulder. I did not say anything, glad that I was home. I sat upright, wondering what I was supposed to do. Mum saw my stiff posture: 'This is your home now, Eric. Let me get you a cup of tea.'

'Yes, please.' But I did not often drink tea, except at meal times. I looked back, to Gran – she was blind and sat still, her thick lenses whirling my vision from getting a still view of her eyes. I stared at the fire, its warmth comforting, and its primal flick of flames settling my agitation. I became sleepy.

'I didn't wake you,' my Mum stated, adding, 'I'll make a fresh pot.'

Sharply, I became awake, a little shocked that I had slept; it took a moment for me to understand where I was – my heart pained, and I wanted to cry. I was glad that she was not looking at my face.

'No, that's all right Mum.' I coughed to clear my feelings. 'Is there anything to eat?'

'Let me get a sandwich.' Mum moved away to the nearby kitchen.

I went to bed early; there seemed nothing else to do, least not this evening.

Mum had put a hot water bottle in the bed, between the flannelette sheets. I felt the dampness outside the area that the bottle warmed. The bedroom air was damp and cool. I cuddled up to myself. Cold and tired, my toes warming up on the squashy water bottle, I fell asleep.

The following day I got up late – ten o'clock. 'Eee, poor lad, the sleep done you good,' Gran told me.

A small Christmas tree was up, its few lights of red glistening. I was happy at its prettiness – and a little sad: it was not like the magnificence of the Homes' Christmas trees.

'This is your home, Eric. You can come here and you can get a job. What do you say?'

Instantly, images of the sunshine, and the gardens, and the crowds of chattering boys filled my mind; and I thought of my horticultural training: all would be lost. Then pictures of the sooty buildings of Preston – the blackened railway here, the clanging of the carriages shunting in the dark still night – for I awoke to this sound before slipping back to sleep, tugged at some deep area of my heart. *No*, my mind said, crushing over the rise of hope and love from my heart. 'No,' I spoke aloud. Mum stood a moment, very still. I did not look at her again, till she moved away to the kitchen, silently. I felt a little pang of sorrow for her but quickly shut this sentiment away; a shadow sensation of regret followed, hesitating over my heart. Gran did not say anything. Though I loved her, for she had raised me till the age of two years; it was her smell and comfort that had given me my germinal sense of "home" – but even her presence was not enough. Yet all this homely place secured a warmth inside me – as if this home *was* mine; because it was my Mum's place, and Gran's too: the snugness of the house and the silent private enclosure of the whitewashed walls of the tiny back yard; Gran's long silver hair, sometimes wispy over her face, sometimes held back; the immediacy of the front door onto the lifeblood of the street, leading onto the thoroughfare of Fishergate Hill. It would all have to remain a stilled picture of a passed dream. And hung on the fireside wall, the small see-through plastic-covered picture of Jesus, his profile looking upwards, through a stream of light, a gift I had bought for my mother from Barrows Green days. On its back, the message: "To Mum. Love Eric xx, 1952". From those years too, I wrote weekly letters to her. Of them I had forgotten. Years afterwards, I realised that Mum had thrown away, destroyed them all. I had written to her as a small child: all on the Home's rubber-stamped addressed, blue-lined paper, some from Liverpool, but most from Barrows Green. She showed them to me on this trip. I gazed at the large plain writing, and the print lettering, of my childhood hand, evenly spaced and clearly written: "Dear Mum, I am well. I hope you are. Love, Eric." But that was gone, even as the house would go, but all that would be several years later, and not to my knowledge, till after Goldings.

I settled into my Christmas home here, and Mum's cooking; the domesticity of it all tickled my curiosity. I had been used to large kitchens, and cooks in white jackets and rows of large aluminium pans; and racks of ladles; of big cupboards – and the wide ovens in the centre of it all. Here, at Mum's house, the small stove, with a few gas burners on top, appeared peculiar.

'You've got a big appetite,' Mum said.

'Eee, he's a big lad, Gladys.' Gran told her. I visualised myself as a strange animal, devouring lots of food, but I did not think I ate much, just enough to fill me.

Gran could not walk out and about; she kept to the house. Mum took me to the market. The bustle of people, the stall holders shouting their wares, and the still lights overhead showed me a different life. The Homes were controlled and organised, we did according to routine and the rules; we did not have to think for ourselves: where our food came from, what lay in the outer world nor what "self-responsibility" meant.

I liked Preston and the friendly atmosphere of the crowds. Back at home, in the evening, I sat on Mum's knee. I wanted to snuggle into her: 'Eric, you are too old for that; you need to get off me.' I was rejected. I could not understand. She was my mother, why did she not cuddle me? I was big, I could see that, but I felt a child inside of me. I was stunned; I could not speak. I lifted myself off of her knees, and moved away to a fireside chair. I vaguely understood that it was too late now for her love. I had needed that cuddle long ago.

The next day I heard, then saw, Gran giving Mum a half-crown piece. She had told Gran of her shortage for the house money. 'Don't worry, Gladys; here, I keep a bit of my blind pension away, if you need it,' as Gran lifted it out of a small worn purse that she had tucked within the deep layers of her clothing. I could see, on Mum's face, her concern, and relief, when Gran had the money to give. It was a new experience for me, watching this gentle exchange of help; it was also a confirmation again of the importance, and the fear, that money had. It appeared to rule Mum's life, least at that moment of need. Otherwise money did not appear again to me in my Christmas-time stay.

On the eve of Christmas Day I went out by myself, climbing easily up the long hill of Fishergate and into the town centre. I was in my own company, and free. The excitement in me of some potential danger appeared to brighten up every face and every lighted shop window. I was looking for something, but I knew not what. Not yet fourteen years of age I was an innocent, an ignorant-of-the-ways-of-the-world Barnardo Boy. The turning off from Fishergate Hill, into Beech Street, was now a long way off. Home and Gran and Mum disappeared from my imagination. Here were the throngs of the early night celebrations.

I joined the mass of folk gathered on the market square. I squeezed forward, and peered toward the centre: there were performers and music, and large lanterns of light to show the scene. The warmth and excitement of the people about me drew my senses, for once, away from my self-conscious mind. I became the crowd.

A moment later, or so it seemed, I darted my eyes across and to the left of me. On the far groupings of people my eyes met the scary, glassy stare of a dark-suited man. He had a black bowler hat on and a ruddy face. I became frightened, his glaring eyes would not leave me; he seemed to be making me naked. I could not understand him but feared he wanted me. *I have to get back home*, entered my mind. I slipped backwards into the rear of the crowd, sidled away from the opposite area of where the black-suited man had stood, and walked quickly off the square and down a side road. I did not look back, but kept going fast down the road, knowing that it would lead to join Fishergate Hill. My adventure had abruptly finished and I was unhappy about it, my fear had taken my joy away. Soon I turned off the hill road and entered Beech Street, its time-worn terraced houses and cobbled way seeming to welcome me. I eagerly tapped at the door of number fifteen. The night was cold but I was hot and breathing heavily. I looked round to the street entrance, fearing I may have been followed: no one there, then Mum opened the door, and I was safe.

'You are back early,' Mum said.

'Yes, it was enough,' I said carefully.

'Did you see the lighted tree and the market square?'

'Yes, it was nice.'

And the few hours before bed passed by. There, with a cocoa drink in my hand, I sat in the quiet company of Gran and Mum. I watched the dancing flames of the coal fire, the rest of the room dim and cool outside the circle of home and hearth.

'Do you want to read "The Post", Eric?' Mum asked softly.

'OK,' I said, a bit curious to look at the local newspaper; the regular reading of it seemed important to Mum. I took the paper: *Lancashire Evening Post* spread its title across the top front page. Glancing through, I saw the paper was full of little stories about people and their lives. It was all a lot of confusing activity for me to take in and imagine, and I soon blocked it out of my mind. 'I've finished it,' I told Mum, and passed it back to her.

Out of the blue, Gran suddenly said: 'You keep wrapped up, going out at night, lad.'

It sounded funny, but I had to pay close attention to her as her voice was soft, and I respected her age – she appeared wise, and a little mysterious, to me.

'It's a good job you don't have to go to the mill, Gladys. Too hard work there for you; and when you had the babies.' Gran was patting the ends of her shawl as she spoke, the crochet-patterned fabric lying on her lap. I watched her closely, each small movement was important for me, as most of the time I only saw her sitting very still – thinking, it appeared.

'I know,' was all Mum replied.

'All those winters you went. You were a good daughter, Gladys, looking after me.' Gran pulled her shawl tighter over her shoulder, a regular thing I saw her do; her long thick silvery hair hanging straight down over her knitted shoulder covering.

'I'll go to bed now,' I said and got up.

'Can you make your bottle, Eric?' Mum asked.

'Yes,' I said and went to the kitchen, taking the rubber one from the wall hook, for Mum used the hard pot one, to warm her bed, wrapping it in cloth, which I did not need to do for my warmer.

In the bedroom I used the potty from under the bed as it was too dark to go to the outside toilet. It was odd to think that toilet lumps floated in the chamber pot throughout the night, till they were emptied in the back yard toilet, in the following morning. It was all such a different set-up from the Homes, where toilets were inside and where we had plenty of bathrooms; Mum's house had no bathroom – we all just washed from a bowl, in the kitchen, in the evenings. Gran had a face wash, was all I saw, and always kept to her bed, in the corner of the living room. At least she had the warmth of the banked up fire, till it died down, through most of the night, whereas my bedroom was damp and cold.

Christmas Day arrived. I cleaned the ashes from the fire and relit it. Mum appreciated me doing this job – I did not mind doing this novel activity at all.

The fire eased the living room into life. The sun did not come into the house, maybe because it was winter time, and so the rooms remained dull, with little light about; the brass or copper gas fittings sticking out from the old paper on the walls had no use in them, light coming from a dim centre ceiling bulb. The small areas of the rooms, which were cold and damp, depressed my spirits. But the warmth of family companionship kept me going. Mum cooked all the Christmas dinner, the kitchen one small room filled with steam and heat, which was totally different from the cool damp of the rest of the house. I imagined that each terraced house along the short street would be the same, even the red polished stone step, at their front doors, looked the same as ours.

A day after Christmas, Mum and I took a walk, and passed by the bottom of Beech Street, where lay Solomon's market garden: 'Your father had a market garden,' she told me suddenly, from her silence. Images of my life in gardening, and coming to Preston, created an uneasy, but not unlikable, feeling inside of me: I could be following my father's footsteps.

Another day we walked slowly up Fishergate; Mum was tall but she moved without haste. We passed by a coal merchant's business. 'It was a poor do for him. He used to deliver coal to us, on his horse cart.' I looked at the neglected sign above the boarding. 'His business failed last winter. He took his own life.' Mum's face was shadowed somehow, as she told me: 'They found him hanging in his shop.' The sombre statement wore heavy on my mind. I shared Mum's sorrow there – and we walked on up the rest of the hill, silently. I was glad that I had not read this story in the *Lancashire Post*. Mum showed me the large open market: it was full of activity, poor-looking people in scruffy clothes poking into the stalls and their products, lifting and peering at this and that: many lots of little things, objects and clothing. I fingered the grubby-worn paperbacks, packed in their rows. I picked up a Hank Janson; its cover of a blonde woman, with her blouse half-opened, attracted my attention. I knew what would be inside, for his books had circulated in the school dorms, and I bought it. I would read it in the damp bedroom tonight, thinking too, at the same time, of some of the boys at Goldings. There were stacks of Leslie Charteris, *The Saint* books; his were of ideal blonde women, unemotional and cold – beautiful, but cold, whereas the Hank Janson female descriptions lowered me to deep stirrings, which I did not understand, maybe that which I feared, of my future.

We passed Sweetman's bookshop. Mum saw me look intently into the display window: 'You could get a job there, Eric. You are smart enough.' But I did not say anything, as was my nature. I feared to reveal to myself that I had feelings of happiness or future hopes and certainly never to mention them to anyone, though Mum's remark was tempting to my imagination, to accept the possibility of work here. For a moment it flashed into my mind again: the comparison of Preston life and the school; the emotional pull of Gran's worn pin cushion, sitting upstairs on the stout chest of drawers, like a silent, half-squashed hedgehog, its aromatic scent drawing me to smell it each time I entered Mum's bedroom; making up the fire in the morning if it had gone out during the night, as it usually did; the cool spaces behind us as we huddled toward the small lighted grate in the evening, my mind lost, gazing into the ever-flickering hiss of the dancing flames. I did not realise what it all meant, yet the poorness of it was such a contrast to the open brightness and plenty of Goldings and its grounds; the sunshine, food, space and companionship; the greenery, the birds, the fresh air; the hope of a future. Here, in Preston, I was enclosed; my future as I imagined it, going to work for Mum, was limited. Here was homely and personal: Mum, Gran and I, but it could not be my place of reality; I had grown through my childhood, too long away from my birth origins.

My brother, Edward, came up but after Christmas day. He was taller and older than me, and seemed very grown up, and appeared to know about things in the outside world of which I had no idea. My life was inside the walls of the Homes. He was not about much – he led his own ways and I did not really notice his presence. Life for him was outside somewhere, not in the house. But his ways were grown up and our minds were quite different: 'Eee, you're like chalk and cheese,' my mum would exclaim throughout his stay. I accepted that he was my "brother"; but having never been in his company, we did not have any emotional connection, or allegiance, to each other.

We quarrelled about who should take the frying pan off the cooker, both of us stubborn about not doing it. Until Gran called out: 'What's that burning? What are you up to?' We, or at least I, sparked up: 'It's all right, Gran.' I dashed to the kitchen, grabbed the pan off the hob and opened the back door. The overheated pan smoke drifted into the tiny whitewashed back yard, where an old wood door sheltered the draughty, and only, toilet.

The day before my last day, while Gran dozed at home, we walked to nearby Avenham and Miller Park. I liked especially the pretty fenced-in rock garden, its small lake and the ornamental wood bridge over it, and the grandeur, as the landscape of the main park swept down to the wide River Ribble. This all felt to be mine, yet I was guilty to acknowledge this to myself: expression of my happiness was a danger I had learnt long ago. I could escape my mind into the large expanse of the fast-flowing river, and over the fields and trees. But really it was all distant to me, just as Mum, though being next to me, was, in emotion, rather distant, but kind; I wanted to be back at Goldings.

So I returned, after a heart-pained hug to my ageing Gran and a shaking of hands with Mum. The return journey I faced with the added emotional experience of my Preston Christmas stay. I quite forgot my brother after parting from the holiday.

17

TEEN WAYS AND
SCHOOL LIFE

"Queen Bee" – First Love.

Once a week, as the evenings got darker, the school had film shows, on a Thursday in the gym; rows and rows of chairs, chock-a-block with our eager faces. *The Fly* film stuck in my imagination, especially the ending as the starry heavens filled up the screen and the human voice, once a man now changed in form to a fly, echoed its thoughts on its life and future existence. And a black and white film, on the animals in a huge forest, of deer standing under shafts of sunlight, awed the viewers to silence. Almost as inspiring were the garish colour films which spoke of the wonders of nature and the universe: *Brought to you from the "Moody Institute of Science"*, as the smooth American male voice told us.

For me, the play and excitement of the winter evenings lay outside: of running about, sneaking in and out of the shadows of the main building, whilst most boys and Masters were in the yellow-light safety of the indoors. This became my personal entertainment. I could see them – watch them, in their play, unsuspecting of being under observation, while I was hidden, and secret, under cover of darkness. The nearby woods though would give a fear to my play, for I could not see into them, nor would venture through their depth of darkness – and soon I would return to the sanctuary of the inside company of the Home.

There were things I did do in the woods, later; but meanwhile, I fell in love, for the first time: with David. He was smaller than me – I was tall and skinny, and he was six months older. I fell for his long eyelashes, his large eyes, his sweet smile, his smart hairstyle and overall his self-assurance as to his place in the run of things. He was secure in the knowledge of who he was; with his lovely eyes and long eyelashes I called him "Queen Bee", my first love. This relationship was a revelation of feeling that I had never known before, and a time, for my first occasion, when I really focused on another person: his whole being was my life – least for the few months (if it really was as long as that, as time whizzed by, yet seemed peculiarly long by the days). Being in love with David also reflected on who I was, made me aware of myself in a different light, and a new worth: I felt more complete. And, now at fourteen years of age, I had my first lessons, by his experience, in kissing. I, a floundering creature, quickly swam to the safe shore of his confident presence. He knew of love, of the habits of teenage sex – and even, I observed in jealousy and shock, flirted with one of the House Masters. They got on well for such a disparity of age and status.

David led me on to further knowledge: 'Bring a blanket. Meet me at seven behind the club room.' This was an adjoining building, like a stone barn, one big room where, in the evening, at weekends, we younger boys could play various board games or entertain ourselves on the piano and smaller musical instruments.

My heart beat fast on this assignment opportunity. I had barely had the chance to kiss him before this night. I was besotted with David, my eyes followed him longingly whenever he came by; I always wanted to be with him. His presence disorientated me. He knew my infatuation, he was in control. His real fish to catch were bigger, for he could entice a House Master to his glamorous net.

I crept through the rhododendron bushes, in the dark. Getting deeper inside them, it was difficult to see, and I stumbled.

'Sssh, quiet,' he said, and I followed him. The glow of yellow light spread onto the small lawn from the activities room windows. The lively chatter and other sounds of play became distant as we moved across a glade and away from any of the buildings.

'Lay down here.'

'Shall we take all our clothes off?' I asked, my heart shaking with anticipation.

'Put the blanket down. Don't make any noise. Take everything off.'

We went totally naked; it was rather cold. I felt awkward as I tried to cuddle his small body.

'Don't do that. I'll show you something. You lie up there. I'll lie opposite. It's called sixty nines.'

We got into position. It seemed odd to me. David's bum was in my face. He, I guess, was facing my dick.

'Lick me,' he instructed.

I felt more awkward. I was cold, David was doing something to my dick and I was trying to get used to the idea of licking his bum. The gentle aroma of his hole was beguiling but the knowledge that this place was the exit place for toilet restricted my enthusiasm.

'Go on,' David encouraged me. I managed a few kisses on his anus but my heart was not in it – and it was a peculiar, new territory for me.

David appeared a bit fed up at my feeble attempts to do as he wanted. I was at a standpoint. I couldn't see where I was to go from here. I had expected cuddles and kisses on the blanket under the rhododendron branches, not this upside-down world.

'We'll have to go soon, before roll call.' David turned round, we both sat up. I saw his stiff dick – it was very long, even if he was a shorter boy than I. My dick was nowhere near his length. Mine wasn't hard; in fact the whole experience, naked on the blanket, had not raised any sensual feeling in me – and I was getting colder.

'Shall we dress?' I asked, feeling regret at the

unaccomplished meeting – our first such like and our last.

'I'll take back the blanket,' David offered – and dressed quickly, lacing up his boots long before I had my clothes on. He left me: 'Be quiet and get back soon.'

In a rustle of leaves he was gone. I slowly tied up my boots. I was betrayed, hurt, used. I was his experiment, not his lover, and this activity had been a strain on my sensibility, but I had gone along with it. The romance was slipping away. I carelessly got out of the bush area and strolled across the lighted lawn. The boys from the playroom were coming out for evening roll call.

'Where you been, Eric? Look at the leaves on you.'

'Wanking in the bushes again?' another voice spoke out from the shadow and light streaks of the clubroom window.

I blushed in the darkness, I couldn't "wank" yet; I did not know the import of that action.

Months later, well past my April birthday, we did meet up again, on a group trip to the countryside of Kent – "The Garden of Eden", my love "Queen Bee" and I kept together. We wandered off and found ourselves in the tall grasses of an old, deserted orchard – the ancient apple trees overhanging about us with spring-time blossom. We came together and kissed in this Eden of Nature.

'Oy! What do you think you're doing here?' A

man's angry voice shouted toward us – though we couldn't see him, our vision full with the thick white blossom. We froze still for a moment, then unclasped and quietly walked away, and out of the orchard; I feeling guilty that we had, somehow, transgressed. This was our last time of being close, together, and touching each other.

On Wimbledon tennis tournament days, as ball boys, we scampered about the stands and explored together, during our break times. Or waited at the small entrance to our changing room, where the tennis balls and things were also kept; the players came to collect such things; we stood and asked them for their autographs, Vic Seixas being one of the autographs I collected, as his Gregory-Peck-featured face, and manly silence on court, I admired, as I did the actor Gregory Peck, at that time.

Travelling on the coach through the crowded London streets, I stared at the turban-dressed men, but I got frightened to keep focusing on each one; I did not want to look out of the window for a time. They held my attraction from the memories of the days reading the particular comics at Barrows Green: the Arab man holding his magic Isis hand-stick with a snake design curled up its shaft, he would say the word, 'Isis' and things would happen.

Though past fourteen years of age, I could easily cry if emotionally hurt, as I did on one of the trips to Wimbledon when Reggie, a boy a year older than me, teased me or told me off about something:

'That's it, cry like a baby then. I've hurt your feelings, have I?' His face was set. He didn't show any kindness toward me in his voice; I let the tears fall down my cheeks and sat there beside him on the coach, trapped in my misery, till we arrived inside the tennis grounds. We all focused then on the spanking-clean cloths covering the small tables, all set up for our lunch, usually of salad and rolls, all of which I was delicately aware, and the polite behaviour shown us by the serving staff, and the quiet and orderly surroundings of the restaurant, seemingly only there for us ball boys. Somehow, and because of Reggie, I had to learn to deny a part of my sensitivity, to protect myself. Maybe this, I reasoned, was what was meant by "growing up".

One such time, a ball boy day, led to my feelings being hurt, again. I was not scampering about in my break period, but dutifully exploring rows of seating after being requested by a House Master to look out for an evening newspaper, to bring back to him. I did not find any, and returned from the day quite innocent about my search activity, after reporting to the Master that I could not find a discarded paper. But the following day, at the morning assembly of the ball boys, before heading off to Wimbledon by special coach, my name was called out: 'Eric Holden, you will not be going to Wimbledon; you were seen scavenging over the spectator stands.'

I was shocked at this public chastisement and even more so by the fact that most of the time I was in the service of one of the Masters. I froze at the speaking out of my name and had no thought to speak up, though confused and frustrated at this mistaken issue of punishment. Reverend Corbett, who organised the ball boys, was a stern character, always seemingly tightly sprung with an aggressive energy, ready to boil over and therefore, for me, a rather frightening person, and here, I did not feel able, nor had the opportunity, to explain what I was doing. That turned out to be the end of my ball boy days, for the following years I was not called out to attend Wimbledon. And I missed the pride of place of ball-boying on the top two courts: Centre Court and No. 1.

Soon after this incident I entered, with other boys, the process of Confirmation; we were instructed, and so prepared ourselves to accept the Eucharist of bread and wine in the school's own small chapel, tucked away in the wooded area not far from the club annexe. This time was gentle and holy for me – then it duly passed, as the expected milestone of our Home lives.

I, as well as David, were choirboys, and attendance in the stalls at service-times was something I eagerly looked forward to: not only for the occasion of the sense of holiness, and the singing, but also for the continuous sight of David, this being the time of my infatuation still, with him. I would gaze at his face as he sang, often losing my singing concentration. My choir days passed away soon and I joined the main congregation of staff and boys on Sunday mornings, accompanied, as the routine was, by the marching with the school band along the yellow gravel path, sometimes meeting up with the chapel through the mist, which shrouded it with mystery from the nearby autumn trees. We were a long caterpillar-line of green blazers, each adorned with the motto: "Finis Coronet Opus" (the end crowns the work) decorated too with small emblems of the trades taught at the school. I was proud of wearing this blazer: it made up, in part, for the ache of not previously possessing the grammar school uniform of only a few years ago.

David and I did not see much of each other in the daytime. In the evenings, sometimes we met, to scamper up house-repair scaffolding or smile in passing on the parade ground. He grew apart from me. I left a note under his pillow, surreptitiously, one Sunday afternoon, with "Love" scrawled over its message, asking him why he now did not take notice of me. Whether he saw it or not, I never knew, as he did not pay attention to me again. Jealously, I noticed that he palled up with Matthew, a tall dark-haired senior. Painfully for me, David, my "Queen Bee", faded from my daily life.

It was not until months after – what with the activities of Christmas, the snow, and the seasonal shifting of new boys into our Aberdeen House, I noticed David had gone. At the back of my mind, I wondered if his absence had anything to do with his relationship with the fair-haired House Master. I never heard, nor mentioned it to anyone. Or, maybe he was old enough to leave – to get an apprenticeship somewhere.

At this time, the song "You Belong to Me" ran through my mind; it reminded me of David, for some reason:

See the pyramids along the Nile,
Watch the sun rise on a tropic isle.

Fly the ocean in a silver plane,
See the jungle when it's wet with rain.

You belong to me.

The sandy pyramids and the snake-like picture of the Nile, and especially, in my imagination, the silver metal shining over the tropical green were vivid to me.

Half a year later I was as tall as the more senior boys: my body was changing. Small, crisp ginger hairs clustered over my pubic area. One afternoon, I delighted in the sight of the sun glinting into the bathroom and reflecting off each small curve of prickly growth, as I raised then lowered my prone body in the re-used water of one of the tubs in the spacious bathing room: 'Look at Holden, the dirty bugger, showing off his dick.'

That was Ronald, a rough senior boy whom I never talked to, instinctively. I was hurt by his remark, and so public, with other boys coming in and out of the room. I kept silent – it was not the truth of the situation. Not looking at anyone, I let my lower body sink under the cover of the dirty bath water.

I wrestled more than previously, with other boys, on our beds in the evenings – in the general excitement and noisy free-for-all before the House Master came around, to check our presence, and if all was okay, to switch off the dormitory lights – thence silence was demanded, and monitored, by the House Prefect, till we appeared to be asleep.

This particular evening, still in my fourteenth year – though birthdays did not mean much to me, as no one celebrated them nor, unless the age date was a particular school milestone, did the Home signify the date to me – I was wrestling with a chubby, blond-haired boy, oddly enough with the same surname as mine, Holden. I was lying on top of him – his belly was bare, his pyjama top unbuttoned, his flesh warm to mine. Unexpectedly, an overwhelming flood of slippery liquid spread over his tummy between us: all my senses were in that moment, and I being hardly conscious of what was happening. The sensation though, was lovely, blissful. I didn't even consider what it was; and only felt the momentary stickiness and added warmth on my stomach. Relaxed in the soft cotton wool of pleasure, I languidly lifted myself off his body. I stepped away from the bed – all in a dream, and moved into my own bed. I lay quiet – and very soon, by lights out, fell asleep. I was not conscious that this was the ejaculation of sperm, and just not being aware anyway, of sperm and sex to create babies, the whole action appeared outside my control, the behaviour natural in its thoughtlessness. It just happened.

Knowing now this pleasure to be had from my dick, and the novelty, that it took me out of my conscious mind, I pursued it. At weekends, when the dormitory was empty of other boys, I would get my pillow, lengthwise, between my legs, as if it were a body, and upon it work my dick, and soon ejaculate. This was my frequent enjoyment in the absent hours of the afternoon; sometimes I did this also when in bed, at night, and I wanted to recreate that first experience of release.

It soon got round in the junior entrance boys (and I was one of them) to the senior floor Houses that, 'Eric can come'. I wasn't in a large social group – I didn't hear the chat. One weekend afternoon I had wandered into another dormitory, an area I did not go often even though the boys there appeared more interesting and attractive than my dormitory. I was looking out of a bay window and Gordon, a short friendly boy, came beside me: 'Can you show me what spunk is like. I mean, how it's done?'

'Lay on the bed there', I said. We moved to the nearest bed and he lay down. I got on top of him, moved myself up and down a couple of times and soon came. I got up and he followed me, back to the bay window. 'Feel through my pocket,' I said. He put his hand in my trouser pocket and through the worn hole made there. His fingers felt on my dick and the spunk wetness around it. We parted company as easily and as casually as we had met up.

I knew boys were aware of my sexual ripening by the individual visits I received: small Johnny from another House, wrestling with me one afternoon when suddenly he had my shorts' flies open – I was sitting on his laid-out body, play-scrapping – and quickly his hot mouth was sucking my dick; this was sex shock number two. The surprise of his action – he seemed competent and used to this routine – did not allow any excitement to raise my dick: and I didn't come.

'Let's go to the ablution block,' I urged, fearing his behaviour could be seen by the other boys in the dormitory.

'No,' he quietly replied.

I stared at him but he was adamant – and said no more. But I couldn't understand why he wouldn't go to a safer place – and, for me, a better place to have sex. I asked again: 'Go on, it'll be better there.'

'No,' he said.

So I abandoned my play on the bed – disappointed and perplexed at his refusal for an opportunity to complete his act.

The next summer Johnny appeared to me in a similar scenario of refusal. We were outside the seniors' club, set as it was in the wooded area, away from the main house, though within sight of the chapel, up the rise of land. Johnny and I were chatting in the garden, beside this long hut. He came closer and bent down; he opened my trousers and began sucking my dick.

'Don't; let's do it in the woods. It's safer,' I told him as casually as I could, not looking directly at him, and hoping no one was seeing us.

'No, here,' he said.

'In the woods, we'll be seen here,' I said urgently, eager still to have sex with him.

'I don't want to do it there.'

I gave up out of fear of being seen by the senior boys who were a window view away from us. I considered later that perhaps the danger of the situation for Johnny – and me – was his particular "high" – it was his added pleasure to pleasuring me and other boys. It became known to me that "sucking off" was Johnny's speciality: "flapper Johnny" was his sex nickname.

There was the Saturday afternoon, in summer time, lolling near Simon in the soft sward of grass strip between the school's open-air swimming pool and the river below us. I don't know how we both happened to be there, together, while most of the other boys were out into town, and a few walking in the grounds, heading out. But separated, in distance and sentiment, from their routine activity, we lay silent.

Fully aware of Simon's presence, yet in my own world, I idly watched one small puffy white cloud. I followed its slow movement, floating above me in the clear blue sky, my reverie pierced now and then by the sharp notes of a startled blackbird whose call marked out the stillness of the afternoon. With these sensations, and the damp smell of the river water filling my nostrils, I grew languid in the fulfilment of the senses; my vision flowed over the form of Simon's bare legs and the need stirred in me to be body to body with him, lying relaxed and quiet, nearby. Then began for me the inward struggle: of the sensuousness of the day and Simon – whom I had ejaculated on at a previous time, when wrestling with him on his bed, was lying now beside me. I, hotly desiring him, yet he, not revealing any need of wanting sex.

'Let's wrestle,' I suggested.

'No, I don't like it,' he quietly replied.

I had to respect him; we being in the same year. Hot and disappointed, I sighed, trying to let my sexual tension go, but I couldn't relax back on the grass. Wondering what to do to release my pent-up sex, I reluctantly got up. Seeing some boys opening up the pool gate, I decided to have a swim, even though it meant lugging through the heat, to get my towel and trunks from indoors.

Another boy, George, with whom I had sex play with at various times, was in the murky green outdoor pool. We met at the side; there were not many other boys swimming that afternoon. 'Let's kiss underwater,' I said to him (with my imagination bordering on the possibility of sex underwater too).

'No,' he replied.

'No one will see, the water's all green,' I said.

'No.' He stuck to his guns.

This refusal I could not understand – but just had to let the opportunity go by. I was unhappy and swam away from him.

Though I had seen George in our dormitory and about, and I liked his looks and lively behaviour, my first sexual meeting with him was during one summery Sunday afternoon.

Being free time most boys were out and about. I had arrived in the dormitory, and sat on my bed for a while. I saw George lying on his bed and I looked at him. He uncovered his body from under his blanket and showed me his naked body. 'Come over,' he said.

I went quickly to him, eager for sex, spontaneously, without reflection. I hurriedly took my top clothes off and, lowering my body, I lay on his body, chest to chest. I luxuriated in his yielding flesh, and delighted in the closeness of his handsome face.

Just then the dormitory door opened and another boy came in: we both knew him, but I did not know this boy as a sex participant. I abruptly left the body of George and began to put on my shirt.

'It's all right,' Tony said, 'Keep on doing it.' I ignored him. My feelings to act had disappeared on the fright of his sudden appearance. 'Go on get back on. I don't mind watching.'

It was too late: I did not trust Tony as I did not know if he had sex with George or anyone else. 'No,' I bluntly said, and made my way to my bed.

His entry had taken away my delicious moment of coming on George.

About a year later George asked me to go to the top field: 'I know a big drain we can climb down into.'

'OK,' I said, and followed him up to the field.

Within a hillock surrounded by trees was the drain cover – a manhole. He lifted the lid off and we climbed down the metal ladder. The place was dark, the floor squashed in mud stuff under our shoes.

'Take your trousers down.' I did and he had sex between my legs, as we both stood there. He came. It happened so quickly. He dressed himself and made his way up the ladder. I was in a stunned state: he had had his sex and just left – there was no emotional feeling from him toward me. I felt used and I pulled up my clothes, feeling the cold air on the wetness between my thighs then the wet muddy trouser bottoms on my legs. I was completely unsatisfied, and though I fancied George a lot over the last year, I had never actually come on him. We separated not many months later: he left the school, being sixteen – but I would meet him, unexpectedly, much later.

There appeared in my early teens no doubt as

regards my feelings and behaviour with the other boys, sexual desire – it came natural, like food and water. I partook as the need arose and, satisfied, thought nothing further of the act. Though of that I later changed, in my late teens, maybe out of guilt of sex, or fear of the outside world approaching – but all that came to a head at the hostel, a few years later.

The Home's life, in the week, was one day of trade training – horticulture, in my case, and four days of general schooling. The rigour and range of school subjects, and the teaching of them, was not in any way near the standard of the secondary modern school which I had previously attended, this school here being provided and operated by the Home in a small bungalow-style building. Some of the teachers did not take particular care or respect for our capabilities. On one school lunchtime, I passed by the staffroom. Standing nearby were two teachers; one of them asked me, 'What is the title of the book you are reading?'

'Jay-o-par-dee,' I replied.

They both laughed. Their response puzzled me even as they walked by and into their staffroom. I later learnt the pronunciation of *Jeopardy*, which was not the same as what I said. I felt cheated then from what should have been the teachers' education of me, though I did improve my writing style, by imitation. But overall, we being Barnardo students, we were second class pupils, it seemed (all of the teachers, except Mr White, the slightly eccentric but very enthusiastic science teacher, left for outside posts latterly: universities or grammar schools).

I did admire one teacher, Mr Smith, for his dark-haired handsome appearance and his smooth style of going about – and that he could speak French. I heard him one school day, when I was passing through an otherwise empty classroom, in lively conversation with the school chaplain. Mr Smith, BA, taught us subjects around English and about things in society. It was his handwriting style which I admired, and I imitated it, in modification, of my own style. I wanted too to have a BA after my name, as I wanted the Rev. at the beginning, like the school's chaplain. I would practise writing my signature with these additions.

We suffered by the general casualness of teaching, as I saw it: attendance in the class always involved at some stage the throwing of the wood-backed blackboard rubber at some boy sitting there – for inattention or some minor talking misdemeanour. Drawing a body in "Hygiene" lesson; hearing a discussion of why film stars get divorced so often – which shocked me, that such a subject as divorce could be open for discussion, from an adult to a child; and the fascinating demonstrations with machinery, and the behaviour of chemicals mixed in glass tubes, were the only highlights of my schooling here.

I learnt the name Jelly Roll Morton, which sounded intriguing: 'Does anyone know what he is well known for?' Everyone was silent; we were ignorant of the name. 'He's a jazz piano player,' Mr Smith told us. We were still silent, not much the wiser for the new knowledge.

The only discovery with maths at this Home was when a House Master, on meeting me and a friend in the school one afternoon, showed us algebra. This was totally new to me and it excited me that letters could also be as numbers in meaning; unfortunately this meeting of informal maths lesson was not repeated, for the Master soon left the Home and the magic algebra letters went with him.

In the organised rush of routine, there was no small corner, except and rarely, the small school library, to have privacy; to rest quietly to read. Though I often carried a book around with me, the spaces of time to read did not always come up conveniently. I was fifteen, and reading gave me some inner stability: I was less agitated, calmer and more secure when in the world of my book. This enabled me to be more objective of the Home life around me. I held close to me my newest find to read *Dracula*. It took my imagination for several evenings, and became a secret world of excitement and strangeness: Jonathan, writing his diary, all alone, filled my thoughts as I too paced up and down the bare stone steps of my castle-like building, and entered the old, wood-panelled hall. Later on, in the summer, I found *Peyton Place* – this warmed up my sensibility, and was a time of emotional discovery, just as it was, in some ways, for its heroine, Allison.

I feared with Allison; I beat with her heartbeat; the school life about me became invisible as I disappeared into her world.

Later on, I was reading World War II true stories, notably the life of Guy Gibson, fighter pilot, and seeing pictures of him, tobacco pipe in hand, posing with his Labrador dog. And wartime prison camp escape stories; all these in dog-eared paperbacks, for I never had the wherewithal to buy them – they just circulated, like other paperbacks, round the reading boys.

Some information on the war disturbed me – enough for me to write a long poem about the "Hun": the longest poem I had written to date, and the first one of such seriousness. The paper with my poem seemed to have got lost, in the usual hurly-burly of school life and with no permanency of secure place for possessions.

At some stage, about this time, I was still in the pubescent whirl of reading Hank Janson – very much dog-eared pages. Simon Templar, the Saint, was reading matter too; both I had re-discovered from Preston Market, when staying at my mum's home, that previous Christmas time. I liked the description of the Saint's women, like goddesses, always just out of reach; I continued being satisfied with these two authors for a while.

The one day training, summer and winter, was for me, in horticulture (gardening, as we boys knew it). Either sweeping up leaves, watching Mr

Wrangles planting spuds or being shown by the head
horticulture instructor, Mr Embleton, on how to take
a fruit tree cutting, slitting the bud of the wanted
variety into the bark layer of a growing variety, also
talking of the process of propagation; the latter
instructor's information I found intriguing. My
interest in plants was very strong – I attended one or
two film showings in an outside horticultural group
of adults. The films were bold in colour and full of
sunshine. The advice was aligned, as I recall, to the
gardening books of W. E. Shewell-Cooper. Though I
was not adept at the physical slog sometimes
required to maintain the smart pathways, or at
working the soil, lifting plants or putting plants in,
or weeding (all this work seemed endless in the
summer heat), I liked to be given information about
plants. I enjoyed the various scented plants of the dry
open air, such as sweet william, its perfume taking
me to my memories of Barrows Green days – of the
colourful borders of asters and sweet williams there.
In the gardens here, the dry powdery soil lifted the
scents with its heat, filling my nose and senses with
pleasure – with the visual life of the orange-walled
enclosure, through the un-gated archway, into the
fruit tree garden, revealing a private paradise,
seemingly, just for me. Occasionally I could tolerate
the claustrophobic mixture of scents filling the
humid greenhouse – though the greenhouse could
also be very dry; the lemon-scented air easing my
nostrils. In the greenhouse there were such a variety

of plants and small shrubs, some colourful, as begonias, or feathery-leafed, as mimosa; and Mr Cartwright, in charge of the greenhouse, always in his cycling shorts, summer and through the coldest winters, with a long nose and permanent dewdrop at its end, hanging there, he telling us what was what, and sometimes requiring us to do a bit of actual work (for he seemed so keen on doing it all himself – but *I* enjoyed just watching him, and being in his suntanned busy company).

Walking to the gardening outhouse, with boots and shorts still, in winter, gave me a thrill. Though cold, I liked the sharp air; that it took me to myself – my very bones. My fingers soon got white and numb, but that was usual with me, in cold weather. Brushing leaves from paths, rotting under snow and sludge, heated me up. I knew that we would soon be called to go inside, for a talk on gardening – or even to go to the greenhouse, to do some tidying of the plant benches and floor.

Near to the main gardening house, as a continuation of the buildings, though lower, like a short row of cottages, the sheet-metal work department had its works. I would hang around there, if possible, in the hope of seeing Bob Peach, though he was senior to me and kept busy in his department. I rarely saw him there; it was in the main school that I occasionally came across him, not at work, metal bashing, as we called it.

On the way to the gardening buildings we passed

the goblin-shaped red-tiled cottage, used by the chaplain. This man, the first of two chaplains during my time at Goldings, was a Welshman. He appeared to me to be holding a furnace of energy within himself. I was a little cautious when going by him. I imagined that he could pounce on me, and breathe fire – even though he was about my height, so short for a grown man, with a Punch and Judy type head. He had about him a bit of the sense of what Mr Clarke, of my Barrows Green days, possessed. I was uneasy and did not trust his presence, though it was his signature I liked to copy (as well as the headmaster's and that of one of the General Teaching staff). He took us ball boys to Wimbledon Tennis Tournament each year – and kept an eye on our ball-boying skills; also on our overall behaviour.

His cottage stood there closed and mysterious. Sometimes, in summer a small girl cycled around its front entrance but she looked sad and forlorn to me. I felt sorry for her and wondered why I never saw her mother with her, or even her father, Rev. S. C. Corbett. Across the path from their cottage grew a small coppice of hazel cobnuts. Rarely would I venture to pick any – nor into the small orchard with the last remaining old trees, to pick fruit, effectively to scrump them. Both food places were too close for comfort to raid.

The wide spread of woods and fields presented my only privacy in a world full of other boys: in the dormitories, at assembly, at dining room attendance, at study and at trade; I naturally spent all of my spare time wandering in the open air. As at my previous Home, I was soon noticed as very much an individual, and a "nature watcher", and so was left to my own way of life. I was sometimes held up as a good example of a well behaved member of the Home. My social passivity was an asset here. I disturbed no one in authority – except that I was tenacious in sticking to my guns if I felt that I was in the right, or for not thinking something was my particular duty, such as the time that I stubbornly refused to sweep the gymnasium floor one day, even though the muscular gym master stood over me. Standing my ground, I passively refused to budge – or speak, and he eventually left me. I had refused to answer him, even his questions, but stood there adamant and silent.

Yet I did what I was instructed to do, usually. I entered the school boxing tournament in one year, though this activity was totally against my nature. I lasted through two competitors till I came up against (as I thought unfair) the next age group up, and the competitor was my friend Robert, which surprised me. I did as best as I could, but I knew he was much stronger than me – his muscles showed that, and after a few punches by him the fight was stopped, and he the winner. Likewise with football: it did not interest me as a sport at all, but on request by the sports master, I did play one game (running about for the full fifty-odd minutes, much to the surprise and admiration of our PT instructor). But I really did not have a clue as to the scheme of play and just kept the ball, if it came in my orbit, in the direction of the opponent's goal. Tennis, lawn and table-top, I liked, as well as swimming. These depended on my individual effort, and so I felt more involved in them; of "teamwork", I was not skilful, and could not think in that shared, collective way.

One sunny afternoon I was picked to join a game of cricket: it was a proper game. I stood, a little out from the wicket fielders. When the ball came my way, at such speed, I did not react to stoop or bend into action. Though I could well judge the direction of the ball and when it would reach me, I merely swayed my leg aside and let the ball travel past me, unheeded. This action of apparent casualness prompted shouts and moans, and 'Why didn't you stop it?' I shrugged: the ball wanted to go where it needed, and with such power that I did not feel to stop its passage. No one again asked me to join a cricket team.

At times, even as an individual, I found that I could not focus my attention and concentrate in any detail, upon any task of new learning.

I felt safer and freer through my imagination, for it had boundless range; my mind could not keep still on one thing. Even seeing the demonstration of the crystal set by one of my peers, and the marvel that a piece of the playground shiny stone material, when connected with wire, could receive radio and let out words and music, did not hold my attention for long; I had no patience to stay with this discovery – to sit and listen. I had to be up and active. I only really settled in myself when alone, in the woods or fields – I felt secure there.

My inability to keep still when in close company with another person came up when offered, by a senior boy, for him to teach me how to play the mandolin. It had a sweet sound, and he knew that I was interested in this musical instrument. But I would flit around and laugh when he beckoned me to sit by him and learn the notes – when he attempted to show me how to place my fingers, to play. I wanted to learn, but I could not ease my internal agitation. I could not be physically close, and settle my mind at the same time. (Sexual behaviour seemed to be in another area of sensitivity all together, and I felt as one with the other person there.)

I sensed safety when in a crowd of other boys yet also held inside of me a space of aloneness. I was an observer – so nature-watching came naturally to me, and was pleasurable in return; to discover for the first time, a tiny, colourful bird, as active as a blue tit, in the needles of a pine tree, and to research it in the *Observer Book of Birds*. To discover that it was a goldcrest was more exciting than meeting up with any new pal or going out to town for a Saturday afternoon's freedom from the Home. Also, to come, at ground level, face to teeth-bared, hissing face, with a feral cat, in the rhododendron bushes, was as captivating as any Home's crowd gathering round, watching a pair of fighting boys.

Some Saturdays I went with others to the local cinema; not the posher one – the Roxy, where coloured photographs of the stars lined the stairway up to the balcony and onto the spacious landing for entry to the seating there, but the smaller, "flea pit" cinema, on the edge of the old castle grounds. If some one of our group paid and went in they would open the exit door, where the toilets were, and let other boys in for free. After the show, or even before, along the nearby street in the Woolworths store, we grabbed a handful of broken biscuits from the display counter – that's if the counter girl was not looking. So we were entertained for the afternoon with this added excitement.

At daily assembly I practised self-control: keeping perfectly still, as we stood during the headmaster's talk; if my face itched, I would not move to rub it, or attend to any other bodily irritation; my mind required control over my body. Likewise, though a year or so later, I practised not to speak unless the conversation was serious enough, as I considered. Chatter or casual talk between peers, I eschewed, only wanting to get, and keep, to the essence of things in life, especially so as I began to read the philosophies of great individuals' lives. I had read somewhere that nuns kept close to the corridor walls when walking, to be inconspicuous and humble; I too sought to be like them, humble. I became aware of the placement of my body when I walked in the centre of corridors, and chose the wall's side. I wanted to practice the abnegation of self. Also, in the presence, alone, of nature, I wanted to take out the effort of consciousness; to join with the sense of the life of vegetation around me. I would be still and sit quietly in the woods, feeling myself into the life-rhythm totality of green plants and trees, flowers and grass. This enclosing gentle force of energy I would sense, my consciousness barely on the boundary of thinking, being in an awareness of the sublime mental peace that I often wished for. Here was the oblivion of self I sought, from a deep aching of my soul, to belong; to lose myself in a greater thing – and this greater thing I knew lay just outside the control of my conscious mind. It was while in this communication, sitting, one Saturday afternoon in the Home's grounds, watching, alone, hidden in nature with my back to the woods, surrounded by the soft pale leaves, with the river below me, that I gained a greater sense of my own being. My heart filled with happiness for tears to come, and fill my eyes.

Such moments were islands of peace amidst the daily rush of Home activity, and the routine of the hour. Even then, I enjoyed times by myself, such as on a summer afternoon, a Saturday again, when most boys were out of the grounds, into town and elsewhere. I had a red piece of chiffon material and wandered by the river, on the field side. I desired to enter the water; it was clear and quite deep. I took off all my clothes and walked carefully into the cold water. The chiffon wrapped around my pubic area. It was sensual bliss: my nakedness caressed by the river, from my thighs, up to my groin. I got out soon, not wanting to be seen, and not daring to fully submerge as I was unsure of the cold effect covering my whole body. I quite often wished and imagined myself naked, in public display like this. Nevertheless, time moved by. I was well into my fifteenth year. I had to think of my future – I could be leaving the Home for the outside world, on my sixteenth birthday; I was worried.

Before that birthday came Robert asked me to town: 'I'll introduce you to a woman; she'll give it to you.'

I know what he means and I agree, following him, a little numb at the portent of such a momentous action.

The day was sunny, and in the open area near the outdoor market, though it was not in use today, Robert casually, brought me face to face with a woman.

'He hasn't had it before,' Robert told her. She smiled; her teeth had noticeable spaces between them; she looked like a gypsy woman, about same year of age or a little above of Robert's age. She gave me a large smile. I liked her, for she attracted me: her sensual upper body just visible above a white lace fringe of a bodice on her black dress. I was stirred to be with her but her sensual draw was too much for me and I backed away.

'He's shy,' she softly told Robert.

I turned away, my body wanting her but a part of me not bold enough. I was unprepared for such a big step. Sideways, I looked at her again: she was still smiling.

'Not to worry, another time.' And her dark eyes lit up as she gave another large smile. She was very friendly and unconcerned about our interaction, and my reticence.

Robert followed after me as I backed further away. The local prostitute turned also. And all three of us left the sunny space and went our own ways. 'She's always here if you want to come again,' Robert told me.

'Yes,' I said, not even contemplating such another possible meeting. Apart from the scare of it, meeting the smiling woman gave me a happy feeling toward the gift which she or another could offer.

In my body there was a hard core of me which could not melt, that was yet inviolable – nevertheless, I felt vulnerable; I feared the unknown spaces that were breaking up on the once-secure line of the horizon of my mind.

That day, thankfully, I returned to the safety of the Home, and its known routines.

18

NEW TRADE: RENEWED PROTECTION

Poetry, Sick Bed and a New Home.

Though I was held up, by one of the senior Housemasters, to another boy, as an example of "Good behaviour; and respectful to staff", my progress report of that particular year, of my fourteenth birthday, considered me a little differently. Ticking various listed categories, none much above "average", the headmaster had summed up:

Eric can do better than this.
Tendency to fool about spoils his standard.

Even so, by the following months, and into the next year, I had quite forgotten this understanding of my behaviour and boldly requested a visit to the headmaster's study: 'I want to change my trade, sir,' I told him, standing as a naked soul under his bespectacled staring eyes. I had seriously, quietly, thought about it during the previous weeks. And how *could* I manage the outside world? I feared it: it was strange – I knew nothing about it; there was an invisible wall that stopped me from moving into that society. Gary had put the thought of trade-changing into my head – as print being a better trade to take up than gardening. I considered this, and the fact that I would have the safety of the Home for several more years, till I was twenty-one.

'The winter time makes gardening harder. I expect you will change your mind when summer arrives.' The headmaster dismisses my request so casually, I am stunned.

'You have good reports this year. You are doing well in horticulture.' He looked through the folder before him on the table: 'Read here.' His thick finger pointed to the bottom of the sheet. I looked:

> Eric has done very well here and is becoming a useful member of the school.

And as instantly I read above it:

> "A" stream boy who has made very good progress.

I looked up: 'Yes, sir.' I was proud of myself and a shade of doubt entered my mind; I wavered in resolve: how can I leave gardening now? This disturbed me.

'Go away and think about it.'

'Yes, sir.' I was disappointed. I hadn't even thought of what summer, or winter, meant working in the gardens; both seasons had their atmosphere, had their different work needs. My feelings were hurt; as if winter was my excuse to get out of the gardening trade. I thought again of my original intent, and clung onto it. I now resolved that when summer came around, I would put in my request again.

'You've done it!' Gary smiled. He was my new trade buddy. Summer was here and the headmaster – seemingly preoccupied with more important issues in his leadership of the school – allowed me to move. Learning another trade – and always within a building, rather than outdoors – appeared a stronger choice. Botany lessons had really interested me, but with only one lesson, I had lost my loyalty to the horticulture department – and the talk of "genes", when I mentioned this exciting knowledge, no one outside the instructor's head had the faintest idea of what I was talking about – and on this I felt lost, and doubted even that I possessed such knowledge. The most I received in reply was: 'You mean trousers, don't you?' I was stumped, and unhappy that my attempt to share my exciting new knowledge had ended here.

In the printing trade, I settled in to a new level of existence. As was usual, I attended general studies school one day a week, and trade practice the four other working days. This trade move led me into a different world: I was introduced to the school magazine, its editing and printing system. I contributed regularly by my seventeenth birthday, with articles on nature, and on photography, supplying my own photographs to illustrate my articles. A poem or two I also added to my contributions over the next few issues, one being:

Creation

The sun comes over the hill
and the earth is still.
Snow glistens white on the ground,
quiet, no sound.

A blackbird sweetly sings
of summer's past things,
then more birds join in
and with joyfulness sing:

so mankind awakes,
destroys, or creates.

The scenes of thick snow crowning the stone arches of the main school entrance, and laden on the crowded trees in the grounds, each winter time awakened fresh in me wonderment and awe. And how it hung on the tree branches, bending them down; and all in silence and purity, such were the grounds at this time of the year in their glistening enchantment.

Going into the side entrance of the main school one afternoon I met up with the headmaster, as he was coming out (not often did we encounter him in our daily passage about the Home). He abruptly questioned me, standing as he was a few steps above me, 'What is it you want to achieve when you leave the school?' I quickly replied: 'A clerk.'

'What!' he exclaimed (much to my surprise), 'they are two a penny!' He did not give me time to explain, for being a clerk I imagined I could write – my writing, for that activity was what I held secretly in my mind to do.

I continued my entry into the school hall, and he went on his way, obviously disappointed by my low ambition.

Later, I understood that he had probably read, or heard of, my school magazine contributions in *The Goldonian*, and was curious at my future intentions.

In my seventeenth year I came down with the flu – half the school had it. I struggled on, not aware I had "the flu" – except that one day, I knew something was wrong with me, and I told myself to go to the sick bay, a bungalow by itself near the main school. In a daze of half-awareness I tapped on the reception outer window: 'I don't feel well,' I told the sister. She looked at me with a stern face then placed a thermometer in my mouth as I stood weakly at the opened window. She looked at the thermometer result and asked me, 'Why didn't you come here sooner?' She was cross – I didn't mind that, as I liked this particular sister; she was kind, though she looked rather like a benign witch with a big pimple on her nose. Immediately I was taken to one of the senior dormitories, they being used as sick bays due to the number of ill boys, the sick bay itself full up. I dreamily changed into pyjamas and climbed into the neatly made bed. I placed my head on the crisp white pillow. I lay there happy, in a peculiar sense of being cared for. I closed my eyes – and from that moment I do not recall anything else – but must have slept, flat out, for many hours; and several days later, recovered my usual health.

During a holiday period an apprentice who had relatives on the Isle of Sheppey took me there. Ian and I enjoyed the freedom of playing on the crumbling clay cliffs along the coast. He watched as I jumped down from high up, bouncing with my feet from each huge clump of clay, downwards, dancing and posing in mid-air as in some musical, before landing further below, at great speed, to the shoreline. This play was joyful, and gave me a sense of losing the constraints of the physicality of my body. (Yet, in contrast, back at the school one lunchtime, while eating our sandwiches by the cricket field, I told another apprentice: 'I would like to be an insect, really small, hidden in the grass'; here, I guess, was another imaginative attempt of getting away, even getting out, of my existence.)

By now, general subjects and school attendance had been completed. I was a full-time apprentice having signed my print indentures papers – along with the headmaster and the master printer of the teaching staff. Till twenty-one years of age I would now have the security of the Home's environment, and I blossomed out a little more, contented in that knowledge.

'Would you like to join the Print Union?' the local secretary asked me.

'I well may,' I told him, unsure about being trapped into anything like a formal-sounding organisation.

'Let me know when you decide.'

I did decide, after thinking about it: I did not like the idea of my individuality being taken away, as into a group, to decide things for me. However, I reasoned the value of being united and so to be strong as a group, and I had a vague sense that it would be right, the working people against some outside force that owned them, or at least, paid for their existence. Gary and the other apprentices appeared to be in the union, though I did not specifically ask them if this was so. So I saw the union representative and told him I would join, which I did. I felt proud to be a member of a trade union.

Like the sports master's request for me to enter the boxing competition, and at another time to play in a game of team football, without my particular desire to do so, I entered the cast of the Christmas pantomime. During rehearsals we had a recording machine; on it I heard my voice. The sound of it was a shock to me. My voice was deep and rough, least to my ears, and not being of the sensitive person I knew myself to be. This put me in a daze, wondering what had happened to me. But I had to accept this change of sound, especially as no one else took any notice. I now had a new image of myself; I was harder in nature than before. *This is how I need to be, to grow up,* I thought, and reluctantly had to let a refinement of my personality go; or, in reality, be repressed. I was Widow Twanky, of "Mother Goose". The part of the young (and rather feminine) boy was originally offered to me, but I rejected it (sensing it to be too much in the nature of who I was, and playing this type of boy in public would reveal my inner self). This role of Widow Twanky was a great success, being mentioned in the next day's morning assembly by the headmaster: 'We were all much surprised by the Widow Twanky. We did not know Eric Holden had such talent hidden in him.' (This comment was followed by assembly laughter.) I felt a little proud – and enjoyed the moment's attention. I sensed I had it in me, prior to the performance; yet to perform with such gusto was a surprise, even to me – but very releasing. I was encouraged by the producer of the pantomime, Mr Newton, also the sports master, to go into the local town's amateur dramatic society. I was reluctant, and shied away. I would need more support than that, just to come out of myself, let alone to enter such a venturesome course of social interaction. My imagination did not open up to any possibilities there. So that potential avenue of freedom for self-growth was not pursued, or opened up for me.

I was feeling more serious with life – and myself; getting older, the other boys appearing childish in their attitudes. The song "Dark Moon" stuck in my mind around this time; it repeated, and repeated the lines, in my head:

Dark moon, away up high up in the sky
Oh, tell me why, oh, tell me why you've lost your
    splendour.
Dark moon, what is the cause, your light withdraws
Is it because, is it because I've lost my love?

Becoming a stranger to my surroundings, I ached to leave this large house. I was a senior boy at the Home now. More than that, I was free of the confines and routines – and daily authority – of the Home staff. I could use the Prefects' Common Room – full of cigarette smoke, manly sex talk and the smack and clash of coloured balls on the large snooker table. It was one day here that Walker, an active, sportsman type of senior, bossed his way to use the table, out of his turn, shoving away another boy. I interceded, arguing that it was unfair of him to behave like that. Walker threatened me: 'Do you want to fight over it then?'

I thought about it – and my mind referred to the time at Barrows Green when, on a similar incident of bullying, by a senior boy toward a junior boy. Though I reasoned with myself how I could overpower him, with the help of some wood lying about the cellar room, I reckoned it would be too dangerous in bodily damage. This senior went to the local grammar school and so I was surprised and unhappy that he did not show fairness in his dealings with the junior, and much smaller, boy. On complaining to him about his unfairness the senior boy threatened me if I interfered further; his conscience not pricking him at all, however wrong he was; and like this present occasion, I, reluctantly, tense with frustration, backed down. Physical fighting was not an activity I willingly engaged in, even as I was unhappy at these situations.

It was not many weeks later that Walker came up to me in the print shop: 'Hey Eric, make one of your headmaster signatures for me. I need this pass signing.' It was known that I could imitate the headmaster's signature in an accurate copy – as well as the chaplain's signature, and the signature of the teacher with the BA after his name.

'No,' I replied.

'Come, you're joking. You can do.'

'No,' I repeated. Walker saw that I was serious. In my mind I would do a signature for fun, but not as an act of deceit.

'Stuff you, then,' Walker shouted at me, inches from my face.

I stood there, not moving away. He then walked off, still cursing me.

It had turned out that he could offer to fight me, as in the snooker room, but he could not beat me at my own kind of strength.

I liked him though, and it stirred in me that I wanted some kind of sex with him but I did not have the wherewithal to step out from my introverted existence and into his male-strong life. Such as in the dungeon-like outdoor printer's toilet I entered to pee. Yet I rarely used it, as the power of the males around deterred me. There was Walker, alongside, peeing. I tensed up and attempted to pee; I could not manage it, and waited there. He finished and did up his trouser belt, which aroused me: on his habit of unbelting his jeans to get his dick out. A small shock came when he zipped up: I did not have a zip as I did not wear jeans, only trousers, and with fly buttons. The sound of the zip movement I found provocative. His sexual energy stirred mine but I could do nothing about it, not daring to transgress his male boundary.

Within this environment, of being a senior boy and having an apprenticeship (and thereby a wage), I was becoming a "young man". Learning the print trade would give me a space to reach out for a meaning in my life – a philosophy by which I could live. Soon after signing my indentures I was transferred to the hostel, the Verney, in the nearby village of Waterford.

I was safe: I would be within the school arena till my apprenticeship completed, at aged twenty-one years. From this secure base, my new life was focused away from the Home – except that I, as the other apprentices, travelled to the print shop within the Home's grounds each work day. Even this attachment, to the main Home, went, as I became involved – or rather, edged into – the society of the local town and into the adult-style routine of the hostel of twelve teenagers, and the Warden's family; the Home and its daily activities was a thing apart now. And this coming period of apprenticeship years would give me an inner stability – which would consolidate, eventually, from halfway house hostel, into lodgings, at age eighteen; and a life with new people, attempting to make my own way into an exciting but strange, new territory.

Notes

1. Accurate transcription? Photocopy is not clear.

2. Workhouse: Establishments where poor adults and families lived and worked: 'children who ended up in the workhouse included "orphans, or deserted children, or bastards, or children of idiots…"' (Roberts, David. 1963. *How Cruel Was The Victorian Poor Law?* Historical Journal, 6, 97-107). NB. The grandmother here listed at times spoke of her fear of 'the workhouse'. Such establishments were operating into the twentieth century; the ethos of such places (their 'value' to the child therein) 'to make them God-fearing, useful and healthy members of society' (*Poor Law Handbook of the Poor Law Officers' Journal* 1901) was much the same thinking and ethos of the Barnardo Homes.

3. Wetting the bed, often recorded as 'Enuresis'. This would be a consistent and major problem during the early years of this new entrant to Barnardo's care and indeed up to his early teen years (an indication of emotional insecurity – the child psychology books would state). NB. Reading 'between the lines', bed wetting was most likely the barring reason for this child being 'not suitable for boarding-out' at age ten (refer to records *Barrows Green House 1 Jan. 1953*).

ACKNOWLEDGEMENTS

Barnardo's (Making Connections) for returning to me my Home's records and encouragement for this writing project; also for permission to quote from my (transcribed) Home's records. Many thanks to Catherine Myers-Antiaye and Paul Sailman of Barnardo's Making Connections team for their support and advice.

Sections of Chapter Four broadcast on BBC Radio Merseyside "First Heard" programme under title *Childhood Landscape* (1975).

Sections of Chapter Four first published in the *Barnardo Guild Messenger* magazine (2009).

Creation first published in *The Goldonian* William Baker Technical School magazine (1957).

Songs:
"And When the Children are Asleep" (*Carousel* musical) Richard Rodgers and Oscar Hammerstein.

"You Belong to Me" (as sung by Jo Stafford) Pee Wee King, Chilton Price, Redd Stewart.

"Dark Moon" (as sung by Bonnie Guitar) Ned Miller.

"If I knew you were comin' I'd have baked a cake" (as sung by Gracie Fields) Al Hoffman, Bob Merrill, Clem Watts.

"Mockingbird Hill" (as sung by Patti Page) George Vaughan Horton.

Many thanks to Ashley Irons for his support and, not least, the use of his London flat for the first draft of this autobiography.

Much appreciation to Ollie for his consistent encouragement, enquiry on progress, support and faith in my writing efforts.

Appreciation too for Gill Tweed who directed me to attempt a story of my childhood.

And Susan Cran for her guidance and helpful suggestions.

My appreciation to Ross Burgess for his editorial advice.

Any mistakes in story or of facts are of my responsibility and are not of intention but by accident.

I apologise in advance to those whom I have not named individually but nevertheless I give my appreciation of their support.

Cover photograph: Ashley Coombe, Eric's second Barnardo Home.